The Encyclopedia of
SURVIVAL
TECHNIQUES

The Encyclopedia of
SURVIVAL
TECHNIQUES

Alexander Stilwell

The Lyons Press

This edition first published 2000 by The Lyons Press

Copyright © 2000 Amber Books Ltd

Printed in Italy

Editorial and design by:
Amber Books
74–77 White Lion Street
London N1 9PF

Project Editor: Brian Burns
Design: Sarah Williams
Illustrations: Tony Randall and Anne Cakebread

10 9 8 7 6 5 4 3 2 1

**Library of Congress Cataloging-in-Publication Data
held on file**

ISBN 1-58574-062-4

Neither the author nor the publishers can accept any responsibility for any loss, injury or damage caused as a result of the use of the survival techniques described in this book, nor for any prosecutions or proceedings brought or instituted against any person or body that may result from using the aforementioned survival techniques.

61369

Contents

Introduction

The shock of being cut off from the regular supports of civilisation – from food, water, shelter, warmth and companionship – will vary according to your circumstances and training. Whatever your background or preparation for the situation in which you find yourself, it is important to get over the initial trauma quickly. Remember that the circumstances you are in are no different to those that men and women have known – and survived – for centuries, even to this day in remote areas throughout the world.

Although you may not be aware of it, you already have the necessary qualities to survive built in – determination, perseverance, ingenuity and humour. All you need to do is to adapt them as quickly as possible to your new circumstances. You may not be used to having to go out and forage for food or to locate sources of water. But remember that the qualities and skills you use in finding and holding down a job, and in negotiating the best deal for yourself and your family in your daily life, are similar to those that men and women have always used to find shelter, warmth and food for themselves and their families.

As you adapt, you will find that if you take sensible precautions in a planned way your body will adjust as far as possible to the environment you are in. Your senses, somewhat dulled by urban comforts, will become sharper and your mind will begin to deal with planning your daily requirements.

If you hold on to your determination to survive, despite setbacks, you will begin to master your environment. By maintaining a positive attitude you will find the necessary will and energy to locate food, water and shelter, and to set about achieving rescue.

A thumbnail guide to survival

If you are cold, wet, hungry and maybe injured, your immediate priorities are to:

- Account for survivors.
- Carry out First Aid.
- Find the right clothing and survival equipment.
- Find shelter.
- Provide warmth, water and food.
- Rest.

You will be in a far better position to cope with your circumstances and plan a survival strategy once you have dealt with these necessities. The order you take them in will depend on your particular environment, and you will find guidance in the appropriate chapters in this book. If you are in a group, you can each be responsible for a task.

No matter how tired you are, set about collecting branches and wood to make a shelter (unless you have other materials to hand), make a fire, and take as much food and water as is appropriate, according to your available supplies. Remember not to eat too much if you have little water.

By constructing a shelter and providing yourself with warmth and sustenance you will greatly improve your morale and your ability to cope. You will also have made it possible to gain much-needed rest, which will make it easier to go about your various tasks.

Do not allow yourself to worry too much about the wider picture, since you will need all your concentration and energy for the immediate priorities. By putting one foot in front of the other and achieving things bit by bit, you will gradually surmount the problem.

Plan for survival

Once you have answered your immediate wants, you will need to decide whether you should stay and wait for rescue, or travel in search of help and civilisation. If you are near a large object such as an aircraft, it will be much easier for rescuers to find you. If you are under a thick jungle canopy, however, you may need to travel so that you can either find a clear area in which to signal from or a place of human habitation.

Location

Try to pinpoint where you are. Are you near any recognised routes? If so, your chances of being found are good. If not, you may wish to consider moving to an area where you are more likely to be found.

Radio equipment

Check to see if there is a working radio, and try to establish contact.

Equipment

Draw up an inventory of equipment in your possession, and also any materials that may come in useful.

Supplies

Check your available supplies of food and water, and ascertain how far you are likely to be able to walk with what you have.

Physical condition

Check your own physical condition and that of others. You may need time to deal with wounds or recover your strength. You will need to weigh this up against the likelihood of being able to find sufficient food and water in the area you are in.

Weather

Do present conditions make it likely that a rescue search could be successfully mounted? If you plan to travel, what does the weather portend? Do you need to wait for better conditions?

Signalling

Check all available signalling equipment and have it ready to use as soon as possible. You do not want to miss your chance if an aeroplane suddenly appears overhead.

How to use this book

The first part of the book is divided into physical types of regions, namely Desert, Sea, Tropics, Polar and Mountain, with an additional chapter on how to cope with Natural Disasters, such as earthquakes and hurricanes. The second part gives more detailed information on particular aspects of survival, such as navigation or firemaking.

Read through the chapter that applies to your environment first. It will give you hints on what your priorities are and how to go about them, such as building shelters and where to find water and food. It also lists dangerous animals to be avoided.

The mental and physical quality that is most required of you as a survivor is endurance. It will not be easy to solve all the problems with which you are faced. Only you can decide on what you can endure. Rely on your training, initiative and God-given skills to solve the rest.

CHAPTER ONE

Preparation and Equipment

Any journey that takes us away from our familiar world, with its easy supplies of water, food, warm clothing and sources of heat, to some extent places us in the survival category.

People travelling by car in a country as populated as the United States have been cut off in blizzards and caught in snow drifts for hours before rescue services could reach them, and no doubt found themselves wishing they had brought more warm drinks, warm clothing, food and water.

Those who set out on long expeditions to remote mountains, deserts or across oceans will be fully aware that they are embarking on a journey of survival and will have made the necessary preparations. Even they, however, may be overconfident of their fitness and the quality of their pack, and may find themselves overstretched or caught out by the variable forces of nature.

However well equipped you may be, it is always best to be aware that chance and accident can place you in a dangerous predicament. The more aware you are of the potential hazards the better prepared you are likely to be to cope with them.

One of the first rules of survival is not to take for granted the methods of transport or organisations you may be relying on. Learn to prepare and equip yourself so that you are one step ahead of the worst eventuality.

PLANNING

The adage that time spent in planning is never wasted applies as much to survival as it does to office work. Simply thinking through a journey in advance, and considering some of the options if things do not work out as scheduled, will be time well spent. You will find that if things do go wrong you will be prepared. You may be able to prevent a good deal of inconvenience, or even save the precious moments that could mean the difference between life and death for yourself and others.

If you are setting out on an expedition that will involve any measure of endurance and exposure to the elements, detailed planning will obviously be necessary. This should be geared to the particular requirements of the environment you will be in. Equipping a vehicle with the right tools, a medical pack and spare food and water is a significant step in the right direction.

EQUIPMENT

Owing to the current vogue for outdoor equipment, the greatest danger is not so much not knowing what to wear or carry but being bewildered by choice and ending up with the wrong equipment. The best approach is to ask trained staff in a specialist shop, many of whom will be outdoor enthusiasts themselves. They will help you to cut through the jungle of rival products and give you straightforward advice on what you require for your particular circumstances. For example, there is an endless range of excellent boots for sale which may leave your mind buzzing, but if you are intending to go mountain climbing the selection can be quickly narrowed down by an expert, saving you time and energy.

One note of caution is that since the fashion industry has adopted the 'outdoor look', you will need to make sure that the clothing and footwear you buy is the real McCoy and not a fashionable imitation.

With regard to clothing in general, the layering system transfers sweat away from the body towards the outside. If you choose your clothing carefully, the material will not absorb the sweat and become wet, cold and uncomfortable.

Headwear

Up to 50 per cent of body heat can be lost through the head, so headwear is an important aspect of your equipment. Make sure you are equipped with at least one sturdy hat. If you are going into a cold environment you will want something along the lines of a balaclava or a hat that can be pulled down to cover the ears and neck. If it is going to be wet you will want something waterproof to supplement the hood of your jacket. In the desert it will be a good idea to follow the example of the Arabs and carry a keffiyeh, or Arab headdress, also known as a shemagh. If you cannot obtain the real thing, carry a piece of light cloth about 3ft 3ins (100cm) square that can be folded to cover the head, neck and shoulders, and wrapped round the face when necessary. These cloths can be obtained from survival shops.

Jackets

A good-quality, breathable jacket is a worthwhile investment. It will help to keep you dry and warm, not only by protecting you from rain but, if it is a breathable material such as Gore-Tex, by reducing the amount of body sweat. That will also help to reduce your water consumption, which is a priority in any climate. The jacket should have a deep hood with a wired peak, storm flaps and large adjustable pockets, to keep your hands warm.

Pullovers

A warm, dry pullover and/or fleece should be available to wear, for example, when you have stopped walking, and should be kept easily accessible in your backpack. Do not wear too much clothing when you are exerting yourself physically, otherwise you will not have anything warm and dry to put on when you need it.

Shirts and t-shirts

Shirts and t-shirts are widely available in materials that are both cool in hot climates and warm in cold ones. Once again, if you are not experienced in this area, or confused by the range of products, ask an expert.

PANTS

You will want pants that are light and comfortable for walking. Another advantage of a light material such as cotton is that the pants will dry more quickly. As long as your upper body is warm, light pants are adequate even in cold, though not extreme, climates. Reinforced knee-covers are advisable. You may also want to consider such features as spare pockets for maps, etc.

In extreme climates you will need specialist pants, such as those designed for desert wear.

Waterproofs

Breathable material is best, but in any case make sure that you will be able to wear waterproofs easily over the rest of your gear without them being tight-fitting. You will want to pull waterproof pants over your boots.

Socks

Good walking socks are easy to find, and depending on the climate and the type of activity, you may want to wear two or more layers of socks. Make sure you have enough spare socks to be able to put on a dry pair when necessary. You will find socks classified under different categories, such as for walking and climbing. Some socks are impregnated with anti-bacterial agents.

Gaiters

These will be necessary in snow and generally help to protect the leather of the boots from damage.

Boots

There is a wide range of boots designed for different climates and uses. Do not just buy the toughest-looking pair, since they may not be suitable for the kind of activity you have in mind. A mountain boot, for example, will not be as flexible as a low-level walking boot. Get advice or read the reviews in specialist magazines.

Ideally, boots should be broken in and adjusted to your feet before you use them in earnest. Consider how many layers of socks you will need to wear, and always try on boots in shops in the afternoon when your feet are warm and expanded. Insoles are an optional extra to consider. If you have leather boots, carry boot wax to keep them waterproof.

The ideal boots will also have waterproof leather and may even have fabric linings such as Gore-Tex, Cordura and Cambrelle, which aid breathability, comfort, warmth and dryness.

Backpack

The backpack you select will depend on the amount of gear you have to carry and the range of your expedition. The principle of carrying a load on your back is that if it is high and close to your body, the weight will be directed more efficiently down to the ground, with the least amount of strain on your shoulders. The further the weight is behind you, the more it will pull back on your shoulders and create pain around the shoulders and neck.

Remember to have items packed in such a way that quick changes of clothing, such as putting on a warm sweater or a dry pair of socks, can be performed without having to rummage around in the pack. Some packs are designed with brightly coloured interiors so that gear is less likely to get lost in a black hole!

Military personnel often wrap items of gear, including boots, in waterproof bags to ensure they are kept dry. In doing this a soldier can even cross a river, using the back pack as a raft, without wetting any gear.

You may want to attach such items as an ice axe; some packs will be fitted with straps and holders for the purpose.

The list in the box below provides a guideline to the range of gear available. What you select from the list will depend on the conditions you will be entering.

Weapons

If you are a servicemen you may be armed with a rifle or pistol, which will give you more options in hunting game, etc. If you are a civilian you will obviously be limited by the hunting and weapon-carrying regulations of the country you are visiting. Never try to enter a country without declaring a weapon. You can carry something relatively light like a catapult that can be kept with your survival pack.

Knives

An effective knife will make life much easier

Survival gear

HEADWEAR	Spare insoles	Sleeping mat
Hat – woolly/thermal/ waterproof/sun	Crampons	Hammock
	Skis	Mosquito net
Headover		Parachute
Balaclava	LOAD-CARRYING	Ropes/cord
Shemagh/keffiyeh/ Arab headdress	EQUIPMENT	Karabiner
	Rucksack	Ice axe
Helmet (for climbing)	Daysack	Telescopic walking/ snow stick
Scarf/neck-cloth (to soak up sweat and control temperature)	Bergen	
		Bungees
	MISCELLANEOUS	Shovel/spade (foldable)
	EQUIPMENT	Compass
CLOTHING	Survival pack	GPS
Jacket/fleece	Medical pack	Watch
Trousers/over-trousers	Mess pack and	Chronograph
Wool sweater	knife/fork/spoon	Heart-rate monitor
Shirts	Water bottle and mug	Torch
Thermal underwear	Survival knife	Dark glasses/shades
Gloves and/or mittens	(length approx.	(especially for polar and
Socks	11¾ins/30cm;	desert regions)
	blade approx. 7ins/18cm)	Monocular
FOOTWEAR	Lockable/retractable knife	Binoculars
Boots – winter/hillwalking	Tent	Telescope
Sandals	Camp bed	Map case
Gaiters	Sleeping bag	Stove
Spare laces	Bivi bag	Wash pack

and it can be used to perform a range of tasks. You can carry a wooden-handled survival knife as well as a knife with a lockable blade. The knife can be used for chopping wood and skinning animals, among other uses.

A blunt knife means more hard work and will consume your precious energy. Use a round stone with a rough and fine grain to sharpen the knife. Make sure the stone is wet.

SURVIVAL PACK

This is an easily portable pack which contains certain survival essentials that will help to keep you going in extremis. It can be stored in a pouch or a tin, the advantage of a tin being that items can be more easily accessed, and the inside of the lid can double as a mirror or reflector.

Typical contents include:

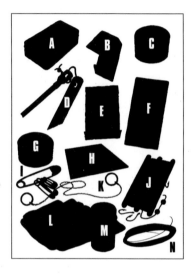

Survival gear

Compass
Flint and steel firelighter
  (you may want to add a
  small cigarette lighter)
Windproof matches
Striker board
Candle (some versions
  are edible)
Magnifying glass
Flexible saw (and/or Swiss
  army knife equipped
  with saw)
Sewing thread (for a quiet
  evening by the fire)
Needles
Single-edged razor
Heliograph (for signalling)
Fishing gear
Wire snare
Cotton wool ball
Whistle
Water bag
Water purification tablets
Bag closures
Wound closures
Antiseptic
Plasters

Sunscreen/insect repellent
Safety pins
Electrolyte concentrate
Pencil
Notepad
Signal flares

MESS PACK

This is what a well-equipped soldier will carry in his backpack. Inside you can pack such items as:

Chocolate
Tea and/or coffee pouches
Milk and sugar pouches
Soup sachets
Chocolate candy
Rice cake
Fluorescent survival bag

The idea is that you should carry gear that will help you in an emergency, especially if you are separated from your main pack for any reason – hence the survival bag.

Key
A Tin box
B Windproof matches
C Candle
D Flint and saw striker
E Sewing kit
F Water purification tablets
G Compass
H Heliograph
I Safety pins
J Fishing kit
K Wire saw
L Water bags
M Potassium permanganate
N Wire snare

Survival pack

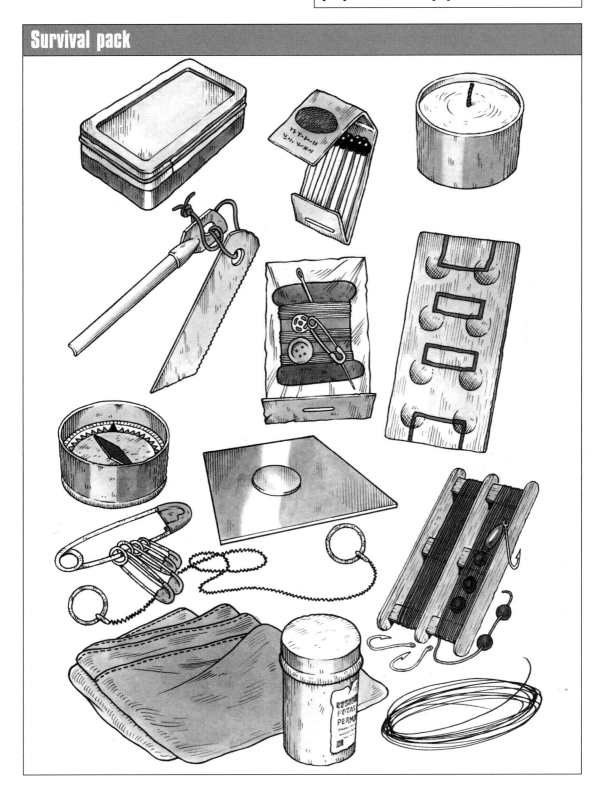

Mess pack and contents

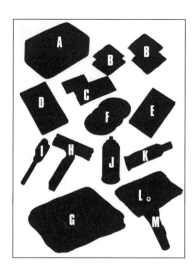

Key
A Mess pack
B Tea and coffee pouches
C Milk and sugar pouches
D Chocolate
E Chocolate candy
F Rice cake
G Fluorescent survival bag
H Half razor
I Half toothbrush
J Mini shaving foam
K Mini toothpaste tube
L Flannel and soap
M Small flashlight

MEDICAL PACK

The following is a guide to some basic items which may come in useful. You may want to add or subtract items, or seek specialist medical advice, depending on the area you will be visiting and the state of your own health. You can obtain commercially available packs adapted to the region you will be visiting, i.e. tropical, temperate, desert or arctic.

Medical pack

Thermometer (you may want to carry a low-reading thermometer)

Gudel airway (this is used to help maintain an open airway when someone is unconscious)

Gauze

Paraffin gauze dressing

Scalpel blades (at least two)

Suture equipment (only carry this if you have been trained how to use it)

Antiseptic swabs (carry at least five for cleaning smaller wounds and blisters)

Large safety pins

Scissors

Green hypodermic needles (carry three for removing splinters and for draining blisters)

Fluid-replacement sachet (this may be a sodium chloride and glucose powder compound for replacing fluids for conditions such as diarrhoea and burns. Alternatively mix 8 teaspoons of sugar and one of salt to a litre of water)

Puritabs (release chlorine to clean water. If the water is cloudy you should filter it first and add an extra tablet. Boiling water is also effective)

Potassium permanganate (anti-fungal/disinfectant)

Analgesics (pain killers): Paracetamol (max dose for adults is 4g in 24 hours) and Ibuprofen (max dose is 1200mg in 24 hours)

Antacid tablets (for indigestion)

Anti-diarrhoeal tablets

Antihistamine tablets

Plasters and wound dressings

Sun cream and lip balm

CHAPTER TWO

Survival in the Desert

The desert is a place of extremes — extreme heat in the day and freezing temperatures during the night. In addition, there are the perils of blinding glare, sandstorms and, of course, little or no water.

There are over fifty major deserts in the world, some of the best known of which are: the Arabian (500,000 square miles/ 1,290,000 square km); the Gobi in Mongolia (400,000 square miles/1,040,000 square km); the Kalahari in southern Africa (200,000 square miles/520,000 square km); the Libyan (650,000 square miles/1,680,000 square km); the Mojave in California (15,000 square miles/38,850 square km); the Rub al-Khali, part of the Arabian Desert (250,000 square miles/650,000 square km); and the Sahara (three million square miles/ 7,770,000 square km).

SAHARA AND LIBYAN DESERTS

The Sahara can be divided into the Western Sahara, the central Ahaggar Mountains and the Tibesti Massif. The Libyan Desert, the most arid region of the Sahara, lies to the east.

The Sahara region as a whole is tableland, the average elevation being about 1300–1600ft (400–500m). Annual precipitation is on average less than 5ins (12.7cm). In the western and central regions, extreme temperatures range between freezing and 130°F (54.4°C). The little vegetation that grows consists of stunted, thorny shrubs, and typical trees are the date palm and acacia. Animals include gazelle, antelope, jackal, fox, badger and hyena. Some artificial oases have been created by digging wells more than 3280ft (1km) deep.

RUB AL-KHALI

Also known as the Empty Quarter, the Rub al-Khali forms the largest area of continuous sand in the world, occupying over one quarter of Saudi Arabia. Salt flats lie in the east.

NAMIB

Situated largely along the south-west African coast of Namibia, the Namib Desert is influenced by the Benguela Current, which keeps the desert cool and dry. Annual precipitation is around 2ins (5cm).

KALAHARI

Inhabited by the Khoikhoi and San peoples, otherwise known as Bushmen, the Kalahari Desert is located mostly in Botswana, bounded by the Orange and Okavango rivers. The terrain has a reddish soil with grasses and brush, while to the east it is mainly sand.

TAKLA MAKAN

North of the Tibetan plateau, and bounded to the north-west by the Tien Shan mountains, lies the Takla Makan Desert, with an area of about 115,000 square miles (300,000 square km). Kashi, on its western edge, is 4255ft (1.297km) above sea level, and the temperature can be over 80°F (27°C) in July.

GOBI

Situated largely in Mongolia, the Gobi Desert mainly consists of a plateau fringed by higher mountains. The terrain is mostly gravel plains. Grass, scrub and thorn cover three-quarters of the area, though the south-east of the Gobi is waterless. There are occasional wells and shallow lakes. The height of the Gobi plateau ranges from

3000ft (914m) above sea level in the east to 5000ft (1.524km) above sea level in the west.

THAR

Situated in north-west India and eastern Pakistan, mostly in the Indian state of Rajasthan, the Thar is about 500 miles (800km) long and about about 300 miles (485km) wide. Annual precipitation is on average 5–10ins (12.7–25.4cm). The terrain consists of sand hills mixed with shrub and rock outcrops.

MOJAVE

Part of the Great Basin in southern California, the Mojave Desert has an area of about 15,000 square miles (38,850 square km).

ATACAMA

Situated in northern Chile, the Atacama is a littoral desert, like the Namib, which runs down a narrow belt between the Andes Mountains and the Pacific Ocean. The area is around 140,000 square miles (363,000 square km). Mean annual precipitation is no more than four inches and the region has little vegetation.

GREAT SANDY DESERT

Situated in north-west Australia and bounded by savannah to the east and west, this is a desert of sand and rock, with a mix of desert vegetation. The temperature is over 90°F (32°C) in January and 50–60°F (10–15°C) in July.

GIBSON DESERT

South of the Great Sandy Desert, the Gibson has an area of about 85,000 square miles (220,000 square km).

GREAT VICTORIA DESERT

South of the Gibson Desert, the Great Victoria has an area of about 250,000 square miles (647,000 square km).

Deserts

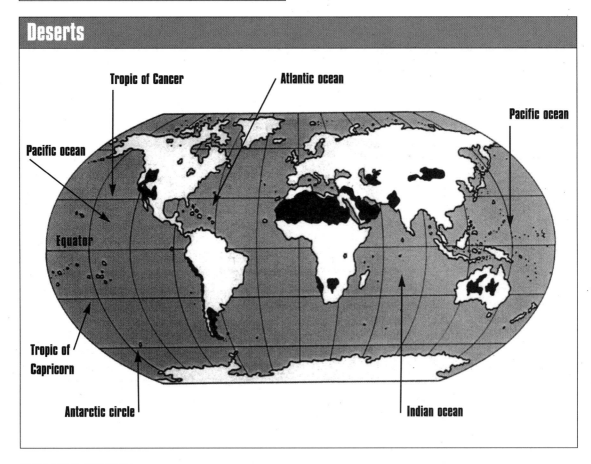

Tropic of Cancer

Atlantic ocean

Pacific ocean

Pacific ocean

Equator

Tropic of Capricorn

Antarctic circle

Indian ocean

SIMPSON DESERT

Located in the Northern Territory of Australia, the Simpson covers 56,000 square miles (145,000 square km).

CLIMATE

Deserts are characterised by less than 10ins (25.4cm) of annual rainfall, an evaporation rate that exceeds precipitation, and a high average temperature. No cultivation is possible and perennial plants are confined to watercourses or other places where water accumulates.

High pressure gives sparse and irregular rain, clear skies, high temperatures, strong winds and intense evaporation. The little rain that falls is unpredictable – the central part of

Maximum temperatures of desert areas

DESERT	TEMPERATURE HIGHS
Sahara	130ºF (54.4ºC)
Namib	88ºF (31ºC)
Kalahari	110–115ºF (43–46ºC)
Takla Makan	70ºF (39ºC)
Gobi	113ºF (45ºC)
Thar	122ºF (50ºC)
Atacama	66ºF (19ºC)

Points to note

- Flash floods may run off the high ground without warning, and thus be life-threatening. This is likely to happen in rocky plateau deserts such as the Golan Heights.
- Sand dunes can be up to 1000ft (300m) high and 15 miles (24km) long.
- Salt marshes should be avoided. They are flat areas where water has evaporated leaving an alkaline deposit.
- Rain erodes sand into canyons and wadis, which can be difficult to traverse.
- Sandstorms are frequent and, apart from being extremely uncomfortable, they can also cause you to lose your bearings.
- Mirages are refractions of light through heated air. The effect they have on objects makes it difficult to assess distances and identify objects.

deserts can receive rain at any time. The lack of moisture in the soil and low humidity in the atmosphere means that most of the sunlight penetrates to the ground. Daytime temperatures can reach 131°F (55°C) in the shade, of which there is little. At night the desert floor radiates the heat back, causing temperatures to drop to near freezing. The temperature range can be as great as 86°F (30°C), and will vary considerably from one season to another. Frosts may occur during winter months.

LAND AND WATER

Since the desert soil is unprotected by vegetation, it is easily eroded by wind and water. Water rushing down from hills can form canyons and large slopes of debris. In turn, these slopes level off to form low basins which fill with water when the rain comes.

Desert terrain varies between mountainous, rocky, sandy, salt marsh and wadi. It is invariably difficult to traverse on foot, and native peoples do not go far in the desert without either a camel or some other means of transport.

PERSONAL CLOTHING

It is a good idea in any environment to follow the example, where possible, of the native people. In North Africa, for example, the Bedouin wear light-coloured, loose-fitting clothing (the hooded cloak is called a burnouse) in order to cover the head and neck to give protection against sun, wind and sand. The air trapped between the clothing and the body acts as extra insulation against heat. Even if traditional clothing is not worn, follow the same principles of protection and insulation.

> Army uniform was abominable when camel-riding or when sitting about on the ground; and the Arab things, which I had learned to manage before the war, were cleaner and more decent in the desert. (*Seven Pillars of Wisdom*, T.E. Lawrence)

FACE AND EYES

A characteristic of the desert is the blinding glare:

> The particles of sand were clean and polished, and they caught the blaze of sun like little diamonds in a reflection so fierce, that after a while I could not endure it. I frowned hard, and pulled the head-cloth forward in a peak over my eyes, and beneath them, too, like a beaver, trying to shut out the heat which rose in glassy waves off the ground, and beat up against my face. (*Seven Pillars of Wisdom*, T.E. Lawrence)

The headdress can be worn to protect the face and eyes by wrapping it round the

face, leaving only a small slit for vision. Additional protection can be provided by sun-glasses or eye covers, improvised from suitable material such as cloth or even bark from a tree.

FEET

The desert floor will be either intensely hot or intensely cold, which can cause blistering of the feet and cracking of the heels:

> The sand was still very cold beneath our feet. Usually, when they are in the Sands during the winter or summer, Arabs wear socks knitted from coarse black hair. None of us owned these socks and our heels were already cracking from the cold. Later these cracks became deeper and very painful. (*Arabian Sands*, Wilfred Thesiger)

Do not attempt to walk barefoot, as it is unlikely that your feet will be hard enough. If you have shoes or boots, ensure that sand is kept out of them by binding cloth, bandage or other material over the top of the footwear and round the ankle. Check footwear regularly to ensure no sand is inside, as the sand will be abrasive on the feet. Also, check for scorpions and other dangerous animals when putting on footwear.

If the footwear is inadequate (e.g. thin-soled) you might be able to improvise an extra layer of protection on the bottom of the shoe (e.g. a piece of rubber) or inside the shoe (e.g. a piece of felt) in order to reduce the heat.

SHELTER

The type of shelter you choose will depend largely on your circumstances and the material you have available. If you are near a crashed plane, for example, it is a good idea to build a shelter near the aircraft as rescuers will be able to spot it relatively easily. Do not shelter inside it in the desert as it is likely to be too hot. First consider the amount of time and energy you have. It is better to build a full shelter in the morning or evening and to improvise temporary shelter during the heat of the day.

SITE OF SHELTER

If you are near rocky outcrops or caves, these may provide suitable shelter, but beware of unwelcome insects, snakes and other animals that may also be sheltering there. Do not construct a shelter in a gully in case there are flash floods. Look out for indentations in the ground which can provide the basis for a shelter.

Types of shelter
Rock outcrop with canvas or other material
Stretch your canvas, poncho or other material from the top of the rocky outcrop to the ground, weighing down each end with stones, sand, etc. Site it in such a way as to minimise the risk of rainwater flowing down the rock and into the shelter.

Sandy area shelter
Either use the side of an existing dune or build a mound of sand. Anchor your material with weights or plenty of sand on top of

the sand bank and extend the material to be anchored at the lower end in the same way.

For either kind of shelter, two layers of material are better than one. Allow a gap of about 16ins (40cm) between them and place some light-coloured material on the outside to reflect the sun's rays.

Underground shelter

This shelter will take more time and should therefore be constructed when the temperature is lower. Find a depression in the ground, a suitable area between rocks or dig a trench up to 25ins (60cm) deep. Make sure that you will be able to lie in the sunken area comfortably and store any

Underground shelter

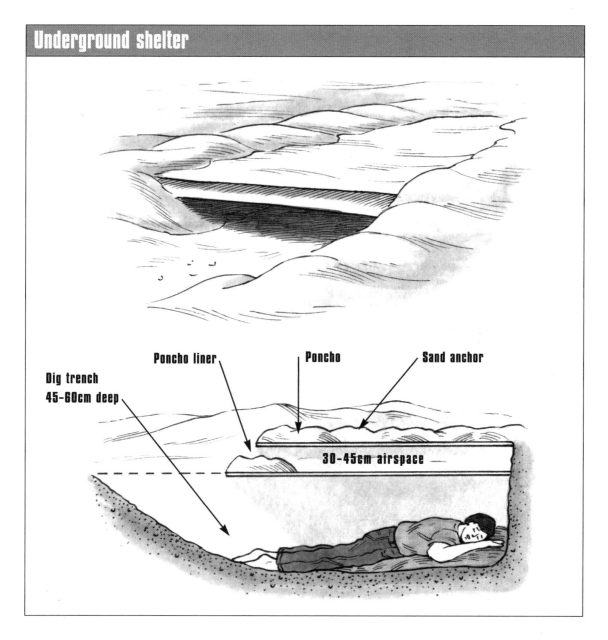

Poncho liner

Poncho

Sand anchor

Dig trench 45–60cm deep

30–45cm airspace

Shelter open on four sides

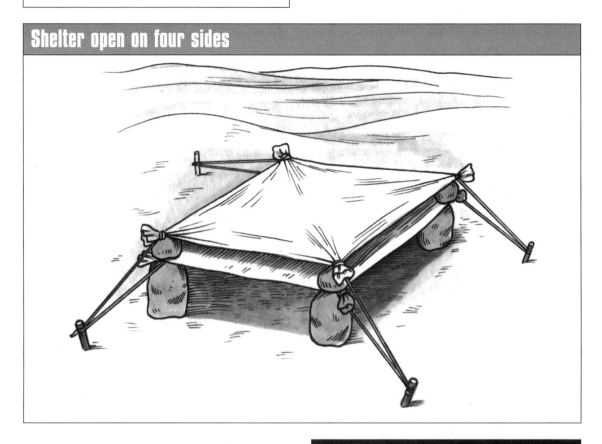

equipment you may have. Place your material over the area. If you have dug a trench, pile the sand round three sides of it to anchor the material, allowing for adequate entry. If you have enough material, place a second layer over the first, with a gap of about 18ins (45cm).

Shelter open on four sides
Similar in principle to the underground shelter, this one is constructed in such a way that all sides are open, i.e. anchored at the four corners of the material.

WATER
In the desert, water definitely comes before food. If you have food but little or no water, eat sparingly until a fresh supply of water has been located, as the food you eat will increase the rate at which your body absorbs

Water intake

Water intake required every 24 hours to maintain water balance during resting conditions:

ºF	°C	US/UK PINTS	LITRES REQUIRED
95°	35°	8½/7	4
90°	32°	6½/5¼	3
80°	27°	2 / 1¾	1

As a rule of thumb, if you have 2US pints/1¾UK pints (1 litre) of water, at a maximum temperature of 110°F (43°C) in the shade, you should last for three and a half days, resting in the shade at all times. If you rest during the day and walk at night (travelling about 25 miles/40km), you should last two and a half days.

Dry river bed

Dig here

Dig here

sweating, breathing and in urine. In a hot climate, as much as an extra 4¼-10¾US pints/3½-8¾UK pints (2-5 litres) of water may be lost, and up to 21¼US pints/17½UK pints (10 litres) if hard physical exertion is involved. When walking in a temperature of over 100°F (38°C), the sweat loss is 2US pints/1¾UK pints (1 litre) per hour.

Foods that are rich in fat require more water to break them down than foods that are rich in carbohydrate or starch and sugar. If you have had the chance to build a shelter, stay inside it during the hottest part of the day, as this will greatly reduce the rate of water loss.

A Bushman of the Kalahari adopts the following method of finding water. He finds the deepest part of an old watercourse, then digs a hole in the sand to arm's length to find moist sand. He takes a tube almost 5ft (1.5m) long, made from the stem of a bush with a soft core, and winds 4ins (10cm) of dry grass lightly round one end. The Bushman then inserts the tube into the hole and packs the sand round it, stamping down the sand with his feet. He sucks on the tube hard for about two minutes, and eventually water comes into his mouth. It should be said that this skill may require a considerable amount of practice to master.

Water can also be extracted from sand or mud by putting it in a cloth and wringing it

water. If water is available, work out a sensible ration. Then drink enough at least to clear the head, which will make it easier to plan how to locate other sources of water.

Dehydration

Even in a temperate climate, a minimum of 3¼US pints/2¾UK pints (1.5 litres) of water is lost by an adult every 24 hours through

Solar still

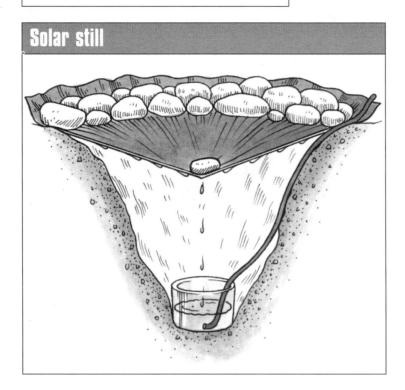

out into a container. During the rainy season, ensure that any rain is caught. This can be done by staking out or suspending a piece of tarpaulin so that water flows to the centre.

Solar still

Dew may form at night in the cooler months. Constructing a solar still is an effective way of catching dew (see below).

Plants that provide water
Cactus

You can cut off the top of a barrel cactus and extract water from the pulp by squeezing or mashing it. Do not eat the pulp, just suck out the juice.

Building a solar still

Materials required:
6ft-square (0.5 m square) clear plastic sheet
Container
Drinking tube
Rock

First dig a round hole approximately 3ft (1m) across and about 2ft (0.6m) deep in an unshaded spot. Dig a further hole for the container at the bottom of the hole – the wider the container, the more water it will catch. Place one end of a tube in the container and pass the other end up to the lip of the hole. Place the plastic sheet over the hole, covering the edges with soil to anchor it. The sheet should droop into the hole about 16ins (40cm), but should rest clear of the container.

   Put a fist-sized stone at the centre of the sheet, directly above the container. Make sure the sheeting does not touch the side of the hole, otherwise the earth will absorb the condensed water. Within 24 hours there should be at least 1US pint/⅞UK pint (0.5 litres) of water in the container, maybe about 2US pints/1¾UK pints (1litre). The distillation makes the water safe to drink. Drink it through the straw.

   One still will not be enough for survival. Three or four are recommended if it is to be the main source of water. The upper surface of the still will catch rainwater, as a bonus.

Finding water

Look for:
- Valleys, gulleys and water courses. Water will normally collect at the lowest point, on the outside of a bend.
- The movement of animals, birds and insects. Follow footprints and animal droppings if necessary.
- Any signs of greenery, especially palm trees.
- Clouds, rain and lightning in the distance – head in that direction.
- The foot of cliffs or rock outcrops. Water may have collected in depressions or holes in the rocks.
- Caves and fissures. Look for any signs of moisture or trickling water that may indicate larger supplies. Use a tube to probe into these areas and suck the water out.
- Any man-made constructions that might mark a well. Look for mounds (formed of hardened animal excrement) that might mark a water hole.
- Water sources sometimes covered by drifted sand in rocky areas. Dig in the areas where water is likely to have collected.
- If you find brackish water which looks unpalatable, find the spring where the water will be fresher.

Date palms
Cut at a lower branch near the base and liquid should ooze from the cut.

Baobab tree
Its large trunk collects water during the rainy season.

Prickly pears
Their fruit and ear-like lobes both contain water.

Saxaul
This large shrub or tree has a spongy bark containing water. If you press substantial amounts of the bark you can tap an important source of water in the desert.

Roots
The bloodwood desert oak and water tree of Australia have roots lying near the surface which can be cut and sucked to provide moisture.

Water purification
Use purification tablets if you have them (in your emergency pack). Boil the water for 10 minutes if you are uncertain of your height above sea level. Add two or three drops of iodine to every 2US pints/1¾UK pints (1 litre) of water and leave to stand for a further 30 minutes.

FOOD
In the desert in particular, food is less of a priority than water, and it is also equally scarce. Check Chapter 10, Trapping, Fishing and Plant Food, for criteria on what plants to avoid, and for the Universal Edibility Test.

Edible plants
Abal
Found in North Africa, the Middle East and desert regions of western India, abal has a broom-like appearance, with green branches producing flowers in spring. The flowers are edible.

Acacia
Mostly native to tropical Africa or Australia, acacia is a spreading, short tree with small leaflets. It has bright yellow balls as flowers and a whitish-grey bark. The young leaves, flowers and pods can be eaten either raw or cooked.

Agave
Found in Central America, the Caribbean and parts of the western deserts of the United States and Mexico, this plant has clusters of thick leaves from which a long flower stalk rises. The flowers and flower-buds can be eaten when cooked.

Agave

Baobab
Found in savannas in Africa, parts of Australia and in Madagascar, its bottle-like trunk can be 29ft 6ins (9m) in diameter. The leaves can be made into soup. The fruit, called monkey bread, can be eaten.

Date palm
Native to North Africa, south-west Asia and India, the trunk is straight and rough, and grows to a height of up to 60ft (18m). The leaves are dark green and the fruit, when ripe, is yellow-orange and contains about 58 per cent sugar and 2 per cent each of fat,

protein and minerals. The leaves can be used for thatching, and the fibre in the leaf stalks can also be useful, e.g. as cordage.

Desert amaranth
The plant appears in many parts of the world. It has alternate leaves and small greenish flowers in clusters at the top of the plant. All parts are edible.

Wild gourd
This plant appears mainly in the subtropical and tropical parts of the world. The leaves are vine-like, and the young ones can be eaten when cooked. The fruit is about the size of an orange. Seeds should be roasted. The flower can be eaten raw. The stems and shoots can be chewed for water.

Wild gourd

Carob
Found in the Mediterranean, Middle East and parts of North Africa, this tree has compound alternate leaves. The seedpods contain round, hard seeds and a sweet pulp. Young, tender pods can be eaten either raw or boiled. Grind the seeds to make them into porridge.

Prickly pear
Found in tropical and subtropical areas, these plants have flat-jointed stems covered with small clusters of stiff hairs. The yellow flowers develop into pear-shaped edible fruits.

Desert animals
Refer to Chapter 10, Trapping, Fishing and Plant Food, for more detailed information on trapping animals.

Insects

Insects are a valuable source of protein and can be found in moist, shady spots, e.g. under rocks, in caves, etc. Take care, since scorpions, snakes and spiders will also shelter in these areas. Remove wings and barbed legs from large insects and take the shell off beetles. They should be cooked before eating to get rid of any parasites. Insect larvae are edible. Insects can be ground into a paste and mixed with vegetation.

Reptiles

These are another good source of protein but beware of the poisonous varieties, which may lurk in shaded areas, caves and caverns. Edible snakes may be found outside in the cooler parts of the day, but only the non-poisonous varieties should be approached, armed with a forked stick and club. Lizards may fall into a solar still.

POISONOUS SNAKES

Americas
Mojave rattlesnake

Deadly poisonous. Found in: Mojave Desert, California; Nevada; Arizona; and Texas and Mexico. Pale or sandy in colour. Diamond-shaped marks bordered by light-coloured scales and bands around the tail. Length: average 2ft 6ins (75cm); maximum 4ft (1.2m).

Western diamondback rattlesnake

Dangerously poisonous. Found in Arizona, south-east California, New Mexico, Oklahoma and Texas. Light, buff colour with darker brown diamond-shaped markings. The tail has thick black and white bands. Length: average 5ft (1.5m); maximum 6ft 6ins (2m).

Africa and Asia
Boomslang

Deadly poisonous. Found in sub-Saharan Africa. Green or brown in colour. Length: average 2ft (60cm); maximum 5ft (1.5m).

Eyptian cobra

Deadly poisonous. Found in Africa, Iraq, Syria and Saudi Arabia. Black, yellow or dark brown with brown crossbands. The head is sometimes black. Length: average 5ft (1.5m); maximum 8ft (2.5m).

Horned desert viper

Dangerously poisonous. Found in Africa, Arabian Peninsula, Iran and Iraq. Pale buff in colour, with a scale over each eye. Length: average 1ft 6ins (45cm); maximum 2ft 6ins (75cm).

McMahon's viper

Dangerously poisonous. Found in West Pakistan and Afghanistan. Sandy buff in colour with dark brown spots on body. Broad nose. Length: average 1ft 6ins (45cm); maximum 3ft (1m).

Palestinian viper

Dangerously poisonous. Found in Israel, Lebanon, Jordan, Syria and Turkey.
Zigzag mark on the back and green to brown in colour.

Puff adder

Dangerously poisonous. Found in Africa, Israel, Jordan, Iraq and Saudi Arabia. Yellowy, light brown or orange, with chevron-shaped, dark brown or black bars. Length: average 4ft (1.2m); maximum 6ft (1.8 m).

Sand viper

Dangerously poisonous. Found in central Africa, Algeria, Chad, Egypt, Nigeria, Northern Sahara and Sudan. Pale with three rows of dark brown spots. Length: average 1ft 6ins (45cm); maximum 2ft (60cm).

Saw-scaled viper

Dangerously poisonous. Found in Africa,

Algeria, Asia, India, Iran, Israel, Jordan, Egypt, Pakistan, Saudi Arabia, Sri Lanka. Light buff in colour with shades of brown, red or grey. The sides are a lighter colour. Usually two dark stripes on the head. Length: average 1ft 6ins (45cm); maximum 2ft (60cm).

Australasia

Death adder
Deadly poisonous. Found in Australia, New Guinea and Moluccas. Colour varies between red, yellow and brown, with dark brown crossbands. Tail black at the end. Length: average 1ft 6ins (45cm); maximum 3ft (90cm).

Taipan
Deadly poisonous. Found in Northern Australia and southern New Guinea. Olive or dark brown in colour, with darker brown head. Length: average 6ft (1.8m); maximum 12ft (3.7m).

Tiger snake
Dangerously poisonous. Found in Australia, Bass Strait Islands, Tasmania and New Guinea. Olive or dark brown in colour, with yellow or olive belly and crossbands. The species in Tasmania is black. Length: average 4ft (1.2m); maximum 6ft (1.8m).

POISONOUS LIZARDS

Gila monster
Poisonous. Found in Arizona, south-east California, New Mexico, Nevada and Utah. Large head and heavy tail. Colour: black mixed with yellow and pink. Length: average 12ins (30cm); maximum 20ins (50cm).

Mexican beaded lizard
Dangerously poisonous. Found in Mexico and Central America. Has either black or pale yellow bands or is entirely black. Length: average 2ft (60cm); maximum 3ft (90cm).

MAMMALS

Like the reptiles, most desert mammals are largely nocturnal. Rodents should be snared with a loop snare when they emerge at dusk or dawn (see Chapter 10, Trapping, Fishing and Plant Food). Animals like the Arabian Oryx will require a great deal of skill with a spear (see Chapter 9, Firemaking, Tools and Equipment) or a good shot with a rifle to bring it down. In the Gobi Desert, herds of antelope can be found. Partridge, quail and bustard frequent water sources in the deserts of Iran and Iraq (see Chapter 10). When looking for animals, keep an eye out for obvious signs such as droppings, tracks, trails and feeding areas.

AILMENTS

Heat cramps
Caused by excessive loss of salt through sweating, cramps normally occur in muscles that are being used, e.g. abdomen, arms and legs. The symptoms are shallow breathing, vomiting and dizziness. Move the patient into shade and provide water with salt dissolved in it (2 tablets per 2US pints/1¾UK pints/1 litre of water).

Heat exhaustion
This is characterised by fatigue, dizziness or nausea due to long exposure to heat; the body may have a temperature below normal and there is persistent sweating. The skin is moist and clammy, the pulse weak. First aid involves cooling the person and providing small sips of water. Heat exhaustion can be accompanied by cramps of the extremities, which should be treated by local massage.

Heatstroke
Humans will die after losing 12–13 per cent of their weight as body water. When the body dries out, the blood becomes more viscous and

cannot circulate around the body adequately. Death from heatstroke occurs when the blood is no longer able to transport the metabolic heat from inside the body to the skin.

Symptoms are: hot, dry skin; no sweat; flushing of the face and feverishness; raised temperature with rapid, strong pulse; severe headache and often vomiting. The victim may become unconsious.

The body temperature must be lowered as soon as possible. Lay the victim in the shade, with the head and shoulders slightly raised. Remove outer clothing, wet inner clothing and fan the patient. If no water is available, dig a trench in the sand and place the victim in the bottom. When the patient is conscious again, provide water with salt added (2 tablets per 2US pints/1¾UK pints/1 litre of water).

First aid must be immediate (see Chapter 6, Survival in Mountains), and the temperature must be brought down to below 102°F (39°C). This can be done by rubbing the victim's skin with cold water or alcohol.

Sunburn

Sunburn can be dangerous if the victim is overexposed. Make sure the body is adequately protected against the sun. Treat using sunbathing/rehydrating cream.

Sore eyes

Soreness can be caused by a mixture of glare and exposure to flying sand. Treat the eyes with boracic ointment and bandage lightly. If no ointment is available, apply a damp bandage. All desert cuts and sores should be treated with antiseptic ointment as soon as possible.

NAVIGATION

Setting course

The desert nights will normally be clear, allowing identification of the Southern Cross, which indicates true south. Once a course has been set, direction should be maintained by compass.

Without a compass, desert navigation is problematic, since there are few features to follow. One method of navigating is to follow objects in direct line with each other, and as far apart as possible. Before one object is reached, a third should be chosen in direct line with the second, and so on.

Assessment of distances

Another difficulty in the desert can be assessing distances. The clear atmosphere makes objects appear closer than they really are. As a rough guide to correction, multiply by three the visual estimation of distance. It will also be necessary to use a more accurate method of determining distance.

Pacing

A proven method of estimating a distance is to measure it through the number of paces taken. The average stride of a man is 2ft 6ins (0.75m), which is 25ft (7.5m), every 10 steps. It is useful to know the length of your own stride, and to practise measuring distances in this way, before embarking on an expedition.

Timing

Another method of estimating distance is by using a watch, working on the knowledge that the average person walks about 2½ miles (4km) per hour. Take care to adjust for difficult terrain, such as deep sand.

You could also combine the two above methods to double-check.

(For a fuller explanation of navigation techniques, see Chapter 11, Navigation and Signalling.)

CHAPTER THREE

Survival at Sea

Oceans comprise about 71 per cent of the world's surface. The sea is also the most dangerous environment for man and, therefore, survival skills in the water allow little room for error.

OCEAN TEMPERATURE

The temperature of surface water in the ocean can range from 79°F (26°C) in tropical regions to 29.5°F (–1.4°C), the freezing point of seawater, in polar regions. Around 50 per cent of total ocean water has temperatures between 29.5°F (1.3°C) and 39°F (3.8°C).

PREPARATION

In survival circumstances it is better to retain clothing when in the water. If abandoning a ship or aircraft, take whatever warm clothing is available as well as easily portable food (chocolate and sweets). Do not jump into the water with an inflated life jacket, as the impact may be dangerous.

IN THE WATER

Once in the water, swim steadily and look out for any floating objects, such as pieces of wood, that will help you to keep afloat. If available, use a life raft.

If you are escaping from a ditched aircraft, swim or paddle upwind, especially if the plane is on fire. Remember, any large object, such as a plane or boat, will create a suction when it sinks beneath the surface which can drag survivors down. Therefore,

The world's oceans and seas

	SQUARE MILES	SQUARE KM
Arctic Ocean	5,426,000	14,056,000
Atlantic Ocean	31,736,000	82,217,000
Indian Ocean	28,364,000	73,481,000
Pacific Ocean	63,838,000	165,384,000
Baltic Sea	163,000	422,000
Hudson Bay	476,000	1,233,300
North Sea	222,000	575,000
Black Sea	178,000	461,000
Mediterranean Sea	967,000	2,505,000
Gulf of Mexico	596,000	1,544,000
Caribbean Sea	750,000	1,943,000
Red Sea	169,000	438,000
Bering Sea	876,000	2,269,000
Sea of Okhotsk	590,000	1,528,000
Sea of Japan	389,000	1,008,000
Yellow Sea	156,000	404,000
East China Sea	482,000	1,248,000
South China Sea	895,000	2,318,000

get away from the plane or boat as soon as possible.

If there is burning oil on the water, attempt to swim under it, using underwater breaststroke (you may need to deflate or discard your life jacket). When you need to come up for air, allow enough time to clear a space in the burning area by pushing the water aside from beneath the surface. Then take in enough breath and, if possible, look to check the shortest route to clear water before submerging again, straight downwards, feet first.

Once clear of immediate danger, practise relaxing by floating on your back with your face above the water. This will allow you to recoup

Crouching position

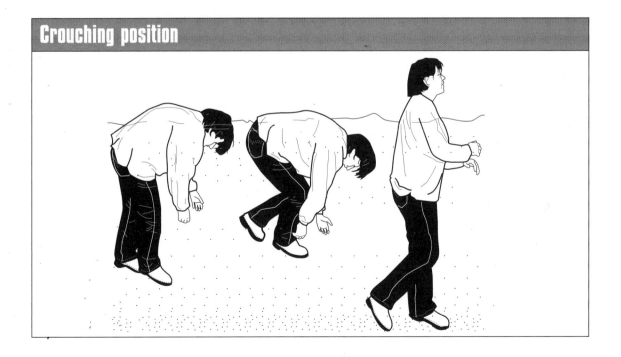

Help posture

cedure periodically as the air is likely to escape gradually.

IN A LIFE RAFT

The immediate priorities are rescue, protection from the elements and water to drink. Observe the following checklist:

- Administer First Aid, giving priority to any wounded survivors. Include dry clothing where possible.
- Check that any signalling equipment is ready to hand, which may include flares, emergency radio and flags. Conserve batteries of signalling equipment, i.e. use only when search aircraft or ships are in range.
- Salvage any useful material that may be floating nearby (it can be tied securely to the dinghy to allow more space inside).
- Ensure that one member of the crew is attached to the life raft with a line, in case it tips over and is blown away.
- Institute water rationing immediately.
- Check for desalting equipment and solar stills.
- Check available supplies of food.
- Follow life raft instructions, such as inflating the floor, putting out a drogue to reduce drift, and closing any sea curtains in the direction of the prevailing wind.
- Paddle towards other dinghies and attach a line of about 25ft (8m).
- Remove wet clothing when appropriate, and dry out. Consider fashioning alternative clothing out of other materials, such as parachute cloth.
- In a cold climate, huddle together to share warmth.
- In a hot climate, keep at least one layer of clothing on to protect the body from direct and reflected sunlight.

RESCUE

The priority is to be seen or find safety such as a landfall. Your chances of being found are greatest if you are close to the area where

energy before swimming again to the nearest life raft or large floating object. If no life raft is available, but you are wearing a life-jacket, adopt the Heat Escaping Lessing Posture (HELP) to conserve as much body warmth as possible. The principle of HELP is keeping the head clear of the water, since most heat is lost through the head and neck.

If you have no buoyancy equipment, you can save energy by relaxing into a crouching position, which will allow your body to float just below the surface of the water, and then move your arms to bring your head up to the surface to breathe before relaxing into the crouch again.

You can also enhance your buoyancy by taking off clothing and using it to create a flotation device. Allow as much air as possible inside the sleeves or legs, and tie the ends to seal them. You will need to repeat the pro-

Life raft and contents

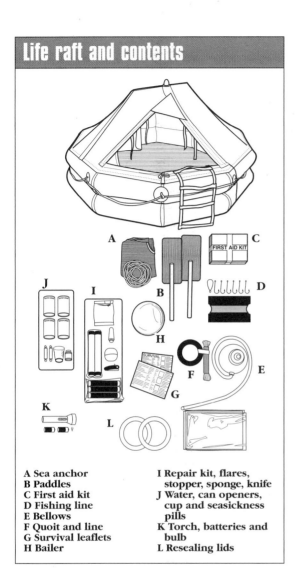

A Sea anchor
B Paddles
C First aid kit
D Fishing line
E Bellows
F Quoit and line
G Survival leaflets
H Bailer
I Repair kit, flares, stopper, sponge, knife
J Water, can openers, cup and seasickness pills
K Torch, batteries and bulb
L Resealing lids

should be carefully protected from the elements, but easily accessible if they need to be used quickly.

- Exercise leadership skills where necessary and allocate tasks (e.g. signaller, navigator, spotter and fisherman). Try to find out who has any specialist skills that might be useful. If you are not the leader, concentrate on carrying out your particular duty effectively and consider the best ways you can do so. Do not interfere with other people's tasks unless asked.
- You will be thinking most clearly in the early stages when you are reasonably well fed and watered, so make plans then that you can remember and follow if things become difficult and you become weaker.
- Put up any permanent signals, such as a flag.
- Work out the best way of using the signalling equipment available in the life raft, following instructions (see also Chapter 11, Navigation and Signalling).
- Keep a log, which records the prevailing winds, weather, currents and state of the crew on board. This will help in such matters as navigation.

FINDING LAND

If rescue has not come or if, for any reason, you consider this to be unlikely (it may be that you are too far out to sea), then attempting to move towards land may be advisable.

The life raft will be moved by a mixture of water current and wind. If the raft is low in the water, the effect of the current will be maximised. If it is high in the water and travelling light, the wind effect will be proportionately greater. Assess which is the most efficient way of making progress. If there is a high wind, it is probably a good idea to bring in the drogue and throw out unnecessary ballast.

Indications of land

- A stationary cumulus cloud is often an

rescuers were last in radio contact. Stay in the area for at least 72 hours to give them a chance to locate you. The following actions will maximise your chances of being rescued:

- Put out a sea anchor in order to stay close to the site. When open, the anchor will help to keep the dinghy in one vicinity. When closed, it will cause the life raft to be pulled along by the current.
- Signalling and navigation equipment

indication of the presence of an island.

- Birds will often be heading towards land in the afternoon and evening. Look out for the particular types of bird and the direction they are flying. If it is the morning, they will most likely be heading away from land.
- A lagoon can create a greenish reflection on the underside of clouds.
- Floating vegetation and pieces of timber may indicate the proximity of land.

An excerpt from *The Kon-Tiki Expedition*, by Thor Heyerdahl, illustrates the possibilities of finding land:

With each day that passed, larger flocks of sea birds came and circled over us aimlessly in all directions. One evening, when the sun was about to sink into the sea, we perceived clearly that the birds had received a violent impetus. They were flying away in a westerly direction without paying any attention to us or the flying fish beneath them. And from the masthead we could see that as they came over they all flew straight on exactly the same course. Perhaps they saw something from up above which we did not see. Perhaps they were flying by instinct. In any case they were flying with a plan, straight home to the nearest island, their breeding-place.

We twisted the steering oar and set our course exactly in the direction in which the birds had disappeared. Even after it was dark we heard the cries of stragglers flying over us against the starry sky on exactly the same course as that which we were now following. It was a wonderful night; the moon was nearly full for the third time in the course of the Kon-Tiki's voyage.

Next day there were still more birds over us, but we did not need to wait for them to show us our way again in the evening. This time we had detected a curious stationary cloud above the horizon. The lonely cloud on the horizon to the southwest did not move; it just rose like a motionless column of smoke while the trade wind clouds drifted by. Cumulonimbus is the Latin name for such clouds. The Polynesians did not know this, but they did know that under such clouds land lay. For when the tropical sun bakes the hot sand, a stream of warm air is created which rises up and causes its vapour content to condense up in the colder strata of air. (Chapter VI, Across the Pacific II)

MAKING A LANDING

Signal if the land is likely to be inhabited and wait for rescuers to come out to you. If you have to make a landing, choose your position carefully, keeping clear of rocks or strong surf. Look for gaps in the surf line. Go round to the lee of the island, where you will be sheltered from the wind. Strong tidal currents may wash you back out to sea, so try to spot a sloping beach where the surf is less strong.

You may be carried along parallel to the beach and some distance out to sea by a rip current, or rip tide. This is a surge of excess sea water escaping from the beach. Do not try to swim or paddle directly against the current. Swim or paddle along with the rip current for a short distance to allow its force to dissipate. Then head back in towards the shore.

Beware of coral reefs in the Pacific – they will be difficult to see from low down in the water. Keep looking out for gaps. Do not get so close that you are sucked on to the reef. If you are negotiating a reef in a raft or dinghy, put out the sea anchor to pull the craft head on to the obstacle. Pull the sea anchor in when you judge the moment is right to take a wave over the reef. Wear shoes and hang on to the craft when going over coral or rocks. When coming in to beach, ride the crest of a large wave and remain in the craft until it is grounded.

Again, in *The Kon-Tiki Expedition*, Thor Heyerdahl wrote:

> We tied the longest rope we had to the home-made anchor and made it fast to the step of the port mast, so that the Kon-Tiki would go into the surf stern first when the anchor was thrown overboard. The anchor itself consisted of empty water cans filled with used wireless batteries and heavy scrap, and solid mangrove-wood sticks projected from it, set crosswise.
>
> Order number one, which came first and last, was: Hold on to the raft! Whatever happened we must hang on tight on board and let the nine great logs take the pressure from the reef. We ourselves had more than enough to do to withstand the weight of the water. If we jumped overboard we should become helpless victims of the suction which would fling us in and out over the sharp corals. (Chapter VII, To the South Sea Islands)

If you have to swim ashore, keep your clothing on and sit in the water with your feet up as protection against rock.

DRINKING WATER

The minimum requirement is 1US pint/¾UK pint (½ litre) a day, though, in some circumstances, a man or woman can live for about 10 days without water. Dos and Don'ts:

- Do not drink for the first 24 hours, or until you have a headache.
- In a hot climate, keep out of direct sunlight and dampen clothes during the day

to keep cool, but do not over-wet or get water in the raft.
- Keep physical exertion to a minimum, especially in the hottest parts of the day.
- If you feel at all seasick, take whatever seasickness tablets are available. Being sick will result in a heavy loss of water.
- Do not be tempted to use sea water for drinking or for mixing with fresh water. It is likely to cause vomiting.
- Alcohol will exacerbate the water deficiency, so do not drink it.
- If there is insufficient water, do not eat, because the food will absorb water from your body. In a hot climate especially, food is secondary to water.
- Look out for rain and make sure you catch it in a tarpaulin and/or other containers. Store as much as possible and drink as much as possible in a steady way so as to avoid vomiting. Allow the body to absorb the water rather than over-filling your stomach. Moisten your lips and mouth before swallowing water.

SOLAR STILL

A life raft may be supplied with a solar still. Read the instructions carefully as the still will not work unless the sea is relatively calm.

ICEBERGS

Old sea ice will have lost much of its saltiness, but new ice will be unpalatable. Old ice can be recognised by its smooth shapes and bluey tinge. Do not approach any berg that is likely to crush the life raft or overturn it suddenly.

FINDING FOOD

It is advisable to eat nothing for as long as possible. Carbohydrate-rich foods, such as chocolate and sweets, if available, could be eaten to offset hunger when water is scarce.

Fish are the obvious source of food, but remember not to eat too much with little water. Fish and seaweed are high in protein, and foods of this type require a comparatively larger amount of body water to digest. Offshore fish are usually safe to eat, whereas inshore fish can be poisonous.

Catching fish

- Protect your hands when holding a fishing line, as well as when holding a fish.
- Use small fish as bait (rig up a net to catch them). They can also be used as food.
- Cut loose any over-large fish and do not fish if sharks may be near.
- Head for large shoals of fish but remember that shark and barracuda may also be present.
- Take care not to puncture the dinghy with fish hooks, etc.
- Fish should be gutted immediately after catching them (see Chapter 10, Trapping, Fishing and Plant Food). Any fish that you will not be eating immediately can be dried in the sun. But do make sure that you have enough water if you are going to eat dried fish.
- In addition to a fishing line, you can also bind a knife to an oar to use as a spear to catch larger fish, though be cautious with regard to the size of the dinghy and a possible capsize or other damage.

Birds

All sea birds are edible. They are best caught either with a diamond-shaped gorge, covered in fish, which can be trailed behind the boat and which gets stuck in their throat or by a noose, similarly camouflaged, with which you may be able to trap their legs.

Seaweed

This should only be eaten if it is firm to the touch and odourless. Do not eat slender, branched varieties of seaweed as they contain irritant acids. Make sure any small sea organisms that may be attached to the seaweed come off before eating.

DANGEROUS SEA LIFE

Sharks

Some sharks are deadly. Beware of all sharks and try to ensure that you do not draw their attention. Sharks can be found in every ocean and sea, and can sense movement as well as blood and other decaying matter, such as vomit. Dos and Don'ts:

- Treat seasickness as soon as possible so as to avoid putting vomit in the water. If you do need to get rid of vomit, throw it as far away as possible behind the raft, so that the current sweeps it away.
- Try to limit the amount of urine or defecation that goes into the water at any one time.
- If you are cut or have been bitten, stem the bleeding as soon as possible.
- If on a dinghy or raft, do not dangle your limbs under the water, and be cautious about underwater repairs of the craft.
- Like most predators, sharks will normally attack an animal that is giving signals of weakness. So if under attack, shouting, slapping the water, kicking or rapping or poking the shark with a stick may be enough to persuade it to turn elsewhere.
- If there are other people in the water, huddle together facing outwards, and beat the water with strong regular strokes. The shark will sense the confidence of the movements.
- Let your adrenalin fuel your anger and not your fear.

Auger or tenebra shell

Dangerously poisonous. Similar to cone shells, though narrower and with a less potent poison.

Tenebra shell

Barracuda

Potentially dangerous. A long fish with a protruding jaw, rather like a large pike. Found in the Atlantic, Indian and Pacific oceans. Length of the great barracuda: up to 6ft (1.8m). Barracuda do not normally attack humans.

Blue-ringed octopus

Deadly poisonous. Found mostly in the Australian barrier reef, they can be greyish-white with blue, ring-like marks. Note that all octopuses can vary their colour, so treat any tropical species with caution. The bite can be lethal.

Cone shell

Deadly poisonous. Mainly found in tropical regions, these cones have a small opening at the narrow end from which the animal can shoot out a poisonous needle that is potentially lethal.

Cone shell

Porcupine fish

Poisonous. Greenish with dark patches on the back, with spiny appearance over upper body and sides. Inflates into a ball when alarmed.

Portuguese Man-of-War

Found mainly in tropical seas, but can drift across to European waters. Floating portion can be as small as 6ins (15cm), but tentacles can be 40ft (12m) long. The sting is painful, though not usually fatal.

Puffer fish

Poisonous. Mottled green with black spots. Inflates into a ball when alarmed.

Rabbitfish

Dangerously poisonous. Mottled green, round, flattened shape, with sharp spines on their fins. Length: about 12ins (30cm). Although this fish is edible, the spines can cause intense pain.

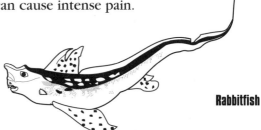

Rabbitfish

Rockfish, Scorpionfish, Lionfish

Dangerously poisonous. Found in the reefs of the Pacific and Indian oceans. Perch-like fish with large spiny heads.

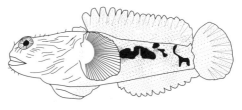

Rockfish

Stingray

Dangerously poisonous. Found usually in warm, shallow water, but also temperate waters in warm seasons. They have a dark, diamond-shape appearance with a long, whip-like tail. The tail can inflict a serious wound. Stingrays are the most common cause of severe fish stings.

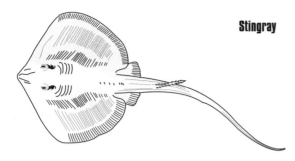

Stingray

Stonefish

Deadly poisonous. Found in the shallow waters of the Pacific and Indian oceans. They live among rocks and coral, and in mud flats and estuaries. Because of their mottled green colour they are very difficult to see. If stepped on, they can inflict an intensely painful, and sometimes fatal, sting.

Stonefish

Swordfish, Marlin, Sailfish, Spearfish

These are all large fish with a spike or spear on the upper jaw. These fish are not normally dangerous, but will react if attacked or wounded. Leave them alone, as the spike could be lethal in a life raft. Wounded swordfish have even been known to attack wooden boats.

Swordfish

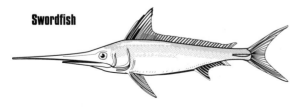

Tang or Surgeonfish

Dangerously poisonous. Tropical water fish with bright blue and green colours. Flat and rounded. Do not be fooled by the pleasant appearance of this fish, as the spines, especially in the tail, can inflict a painful sting.

Toadfish

Dangerously poisonous. It looks like a cross between a toad and a fish, and lurks in mud in the winter. They can also be found in both shallow and deep water. Sharp spines near the gills and first dorsal fin can inflict a painful sting.

Toadfish

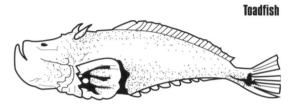

Triggerfish

Poisonous. Can be dark with algae-like greenish patches on the side and underbelly, and stout dorsal spines.

Tuna

Potentially dangerous. A large tuna fish can bite the head off a dolphin, so if you are in a small craft treat them with caution, even though they are good to eat.

Weeverfish

Dangerously poisonous. Long-bodied fish (about 1ft/30cm) that tend to bury themselves in sand. Their mouths are large and upwardly slanted, with eyes on the top of their heads. They have poisonous spines in the fins which deliver a painful sting.

In general, be careful of fish that inhabit lagoons and reefs, and in particular of fish with small, parrot-like mouths and small belly fins.

NAVIGATION AT SEA

If you are in a properly equipped life raft, it should contain navigation equipment with instructions. If you do not have the usual equipment, such as a compass or sextant, the following points may help:

Sun rise method

The sun rises in the east and sets in the west. If you are north of latitude 23.5°N, the sun will pass south of you. If you are south of latitude 23.5°S, the sun will pass north of you. If you are between these two latitudes, the sun's path varies according to the time of year.

Use the table to estimate your position according to the direction in which the sun rises at certain times of year.

Watch method

Between sunrise and sunset, and north and south of the latitudes shown in the table – N at 60° and S at 30° S, you can gain a rough estimate of direction by using your watch. Aim the hour hand at the sun. The point half way between the hour hand and twelve o'clock will show the approximate direction of true south if you are in the northern hemisphere, and the approximate direction of true north if you are in the southern hemisphere. However, if you are in the tropics, i.e. between 23.5°N and 23.5°S, this method is unreliable.

Stars

The night stars are a reliable guide and have been used by navigators for thousands of years. The key navigational aid in the northern hemisphere involves Polaris (North Star), which stands over the North Pole. Polaris is part of a faint constellation known as Ursa Minor (Little Bear), or Little Dipper, and can be identified in the sky by following a line through the two brightest stars of the constellation known as Ursa Major (Great Bear), or Big Dipper (see Chapter 11, Navigation and Signalling).

Without a sextant and navigation tables you will only be able to get a very approximate idea of your latitude by measuring the angle of the North Star over the horizon. A five-degree margin of error in the angle could put you out by 300 nautical miles.

In the southern hemisphere a constellation known as the Southern Cross is used as a guide. The four brightest stars form a cross tilting to the side. Follow the axis of the two furthest apart and continue an imaginary line five times the length of this axis. At about the point where this imaginary line ends, you will find south.

WEATHER AT SEA

Sailors are acutely aware of signs that indicate which way the weather is likely to turn. Two good indicators are the wind and the

Sunrise table

LATITUDE	21 MARCH	5 MAY	22 JUNE	9 AUG	23 SEPT	7 NOV	22 DEC	5 FEB
60°North	89	55	37	55	89	122	140	122
30°North	90	71	63	71	90	108	116	108
0°Equator	90	74	67	74	90	106	113	106
30°South	90	72	64	72	90	104	117	109

clouds. By recognising the direction and changes of wind, the types of cloud and the likely weather they indicate, you can prepare better for either good or bad weather.

Winds

At low levels, winds flow around regions of relatively low pressure (cyclones) and high pressure (anti-cyclones). Winds flow anticlockwise around lows in the northern hemisphere, and clockwise in the southern hemisphere. Wind systems rotate in the opposite direction around the centres of high pressure.

Lying approximately between latitudes 10°S and 10°N is an area of low pressure and hot air. This area is known as the Doldrums. On the edge of the Doldrums, winds rise to create towering cumulonimbus clouds and heavy rain. At latitudes 30°N and 30°S from the equator there are high-pressure belts of light variable winds. The air moving from these latitudes towards the Doldrums is known as the trade winds, or the prevailing winds of the lower latitudes.

In the northern hemisphere, the prevailing wind that flows from the north, southwards to

Prevailing winds

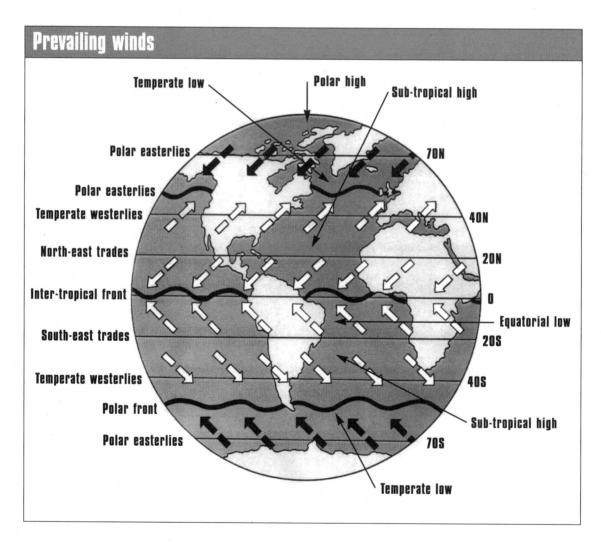

the equator is called the north-east trade wind. It is not a straight north–south flow because of deflection by the rotation of the earth. The corresponding wind in the southern hemisphere is called the south-east trade wind.

In the middle latitudes, the winds are called the prevailing westerlies, though their direction can be affected daily by a number of factors. During the summer, the land continents are areas of low pressure, attracting winds in from the colder oceans. In the winter, the continents have high pressure, and winds flow towards the warmer oceans.

Local winds
In the summer, in particular, the land is warmer than the sea during the day, but it is colder than the sea at night. Breezes thus flow from the sea into the land during the day, and flow out from the land towards the sea at night. This phenomenon occurs across a band of up to 30 miles (50km) width, over land and sea.

Ocean currents
The prevailing winds affect the ocean currents, which are seen in the map below.

Clouds
Four main groups are categorised on the basis of height above the earth.

1. Cirrus
Usually about 4 miles (6 km) above the earth, Cirrus clouds are composed of ice particles. They are feathery and elongated, and

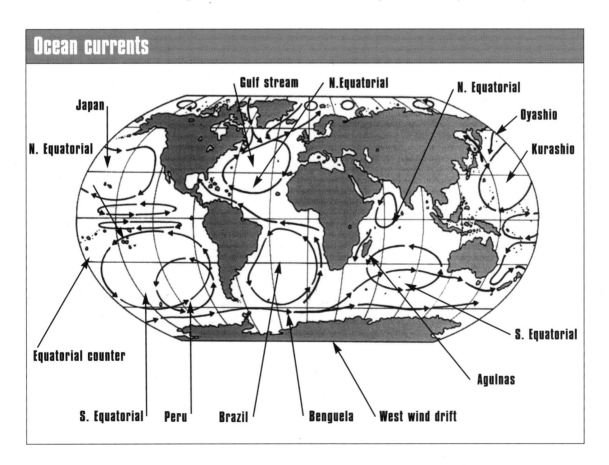

Ocean currents

Gulf stream · N.Equatorial · N. Equatorial · Japan · Oyashio · N. Equatorial · Kurashio · Equatorial counter · S. Equatorial · S. Equatorial · Peru · Brazil · Benguela · West wind drift · Agulnas

41

The Beaufort Scale

DESCRIPTION & WIND SPEED (KNOTS)	LAND SIGNS	SEA SIGNS
0 Calm (less than 1)	Smoke rises vertically. Leaves do not stir.	
1 Light air (1–3)	Smoke drifts. Wind vanes are still.	
2 Light breeze (4–6)	Wind on face. Rustling leaves. Vanes move.	
3 Gentle breeze (7–10)	Light flags extended. Leaves in motion.	Small waves (average wave height 2ft/0.6m)
4 Moderate breeze (11–16)	Small branches moving. Dust raised.	Small waves, some with white crests (average wave height 3ft 3ins/1m) height
5 Fresh breeze (17–21)	Small trees sway. Tops of trees move.	White horses and spray off tops of waves (average wave height 6ft/1.8m)
6 Strong breeze (22–27)	Large branches in motion. Whistling wires.	
7 Near gale (28–33)	Trees in motion. Walkers buffeted.	Seas piling up. Foam (average wave height 13ft/4m)
8 Gale (34–40)	Twigs broken off trees. Difficult to walk.	
9 Strong gale (41–47)	Chimney pots and slates fall.	Waves high with dense foam (average wave height 23ft/7m)
10+ Storm (48+)	Trees uprooted.	Very high waves, large expanses of froth, edges of all waves turned to foam (average wave height 37ft/11.3m)

Cloud types

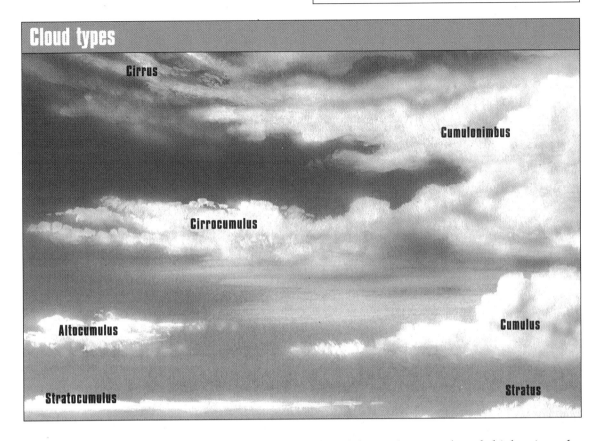

appear as bands. They are known as mare's tails. These clouds can often indicate fine weather, but when they are accompanied by a regular north wind in cold climates, they sometimes precede a blizzard.

Cirrostratus
This consists of a fine veil of whitish clouds, darker than cirrus. When cirrostratus follows cirrus across the sky, bad weather may be about to come.

Cirrocumulus
Small white balls arranged in groups, these clouds indicate good weather.

2. Cumulus
Fluffy, white and heaped together, these clouds are often indicators of fine weather, and can appear around midday on a sunny day. If they pile up and push higher into the atmosphere they can become storm clouds.

3. Nimbus
Clouds of uniform greyness extend over the whole sky.

Cumulonimbus
Towering into the atmosphere, these clouds are dark with flat bases and rounded tops. Sometimes they form an anvil shape at the top, looking like cirrus. They often mean sudden heavy showers of rain, snow or hail. If a thunderstorm occurs, you can expect a strong wind from the direction of the storm as well as a rapid drop in temperature.

4.Stratus
Low clouds composed of water droplets

Boarding a life raft, A, B and C

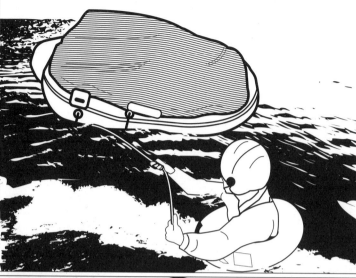

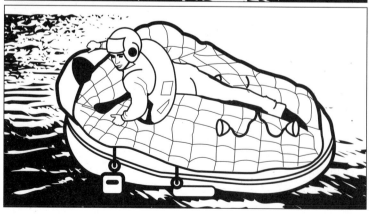

make up an even, grey layer of cloud. They inevitably mean rain or snow.

Altostratus
Holes in this layer mean that the weather may not be too bad.

Nimbostratus
These rain-bearing clouds have a low base and consist of thick layers.

BOARDING A LIFE RAFT
If the raft is attached to you with a rope, pull the raft towards you (A). If it is upside down in the water, pull it the right way up by moving to the side opposite to where the lanyard is attached and pulling it over, placing your feet against the raft if necessary, or by grabbing handles at the opposite side from where you are in the water and pulling it over.

To board the raft, you can attach your inflatable life-preserver either to yourself or the raft before removing it. Then grab handles on each side of the raft and pull yourself in, while kicking with your legs in the water (B and C).

Another way of boarding is to get one knee inside the raft and pull yourself forward into it as shown in D and E.

When you are in the raft, make sure it is fully inflated and check for any leaks.

Boarding a life raft, D and E

CHAPTER FOUR

Survival in the Tropics

The tropics present hazards in the form of infested swamps, bushfire, poisonous plants and deadly wildlife, but are rich with nutritious vegetation, hidden sources of water and possibilities for shelter.

TYPES OF TROPICAL REGION

Rainforest

More than 6ft (180cm) of annual precipitation and a hot, steamy climate are the conditions of a tropical rainforest, which produces the most diverse vegetation types in the world. Typical rainforests occur in South and Central America, West and Central Africa, Indonesia, parts of South-East Asia, and in tropical Australia.

Temperatures are both even and high, with mean monthly temperatures between 24° and 28°C. This is because the upper layers of tree canopies and lower layers of branches filter sunlight and reduce wind movement. The forest normally has three layers of tree crowns: the highest forms the forest canopy; below this is a layer of young trees, shrubs, large herbs and lianas; and a third layer, of tree branches, twigs and foliage, lies just above ground level. The forest floor is clearer than is usually thought, with a layer of humus and fallen leaves. Humidity is very high near the forest floor, but more variable near the canopy.

There are mountainous regions in all major areas of rainforest and increases in altitude are matched by increases in rainfall.

Tropical rainforests

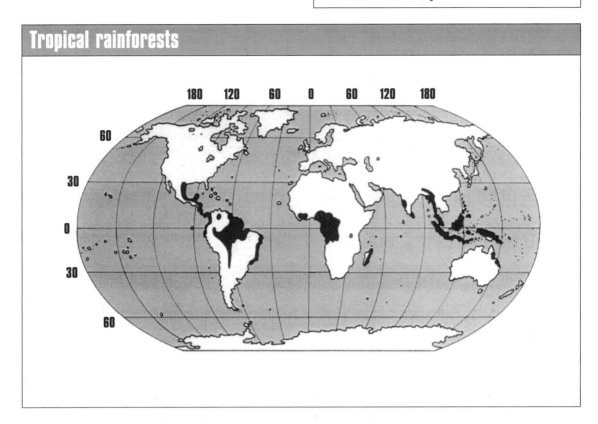

Primary and secondary jungle

Primary jungle is typified by tall trees and layers of vegetation below, as described above. Secondary jungle results from the clearance of primary jungle for cultivation by man. The jungle eventually reclaims an abandoned cultivated area, but instead of tall trees there is a mixture of dense undergrowth and creepers, making this kind of jungle more difficult to cross.

Monsoon forest

Also called dry, or tropical deciduous, forest, the monsoon forest has trees that shed their leaves in the dry season. This type of forest is most evident in South-East Asia and is characterised by teak trees and bamboo thickets.

Savanna

Savanna is found in tropical regions around 8° to 20° from the equator. Mean annual precipitation is somewhere in the region of 31–59ins (800–1500mm), and rain falls in about October to March in the southern hemisphere and April to September in the northern. Mean monthly temperatures are between 50°F (10°C) and 68°F (20°C) in the dry season; 68°F (20°C) and 86°F (30°C) in the wet season.

Savanna is characterised by continuous grass cover, but it can vary according to the density of trees and shrubs. There are categories of woodland, tree, shrub and grass savanna. Bushfires are common in the dry season, and are influenced by human activity.

Mangrove swamps

Mangroves develop in both tropical and sub-tropical regions, and can be found in the river deltas of the Amazon, Mekong, Congo, and Ganges. Many of the animals that populate these areas are dangerous or unpleasant, such as leeches, stinging insects, crocodiles and caimans.

Savannas

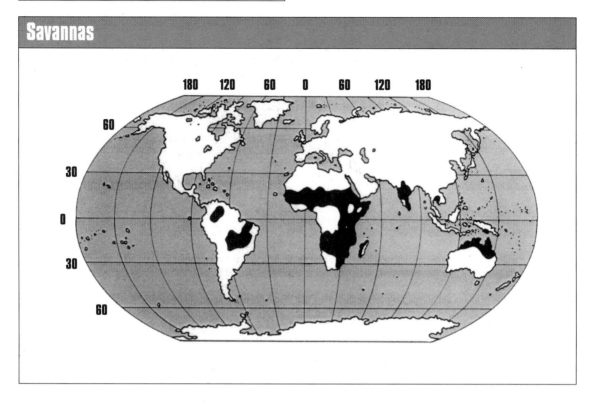

Freshwater swamps

Found inland, freshwater swamps are mostly near rivers that supply the water for them. The water flows slowly through the abundant vegetation, and these areas are difficult to navigate. Tropical swamps include sedges, such as papyrus, as well as trees such as palms.

Personal clothing

An environment with close, often thorny, vegetation and a vast range of insects as well as leeches demands strong clothing. Thick trousers and strong shirts are recommended, as well as plenty of clean changes of socks. Weight considerations may mean it is not possible to take more than two changes of clothing (not including socks), in which case it is advisable to keep one dry set sealed up in waterproof bags to change into at the end of journeys and for night wear. Due to the humidity, clothes are unlikely to dry soon enough, so it is better to change back into the wet kit for the next journey.

There is a wide range of strong, specially adapted jungle boots on the market. As in desert environments, it is crucially important to check footwear and other clothing for insects before putting them on. Powder your body with zinc talcum powder and use insect repellent on your body and socks to keep leeches, mosquitoes and a host of other undesirable creatures at bay.

SHELTER

In tropical regions it is important to be aware of the possibility of flooding, so find high ground and/or an area where there is no evidence of previous flooding, such as silt. Make sure there is no dead wood above or immediately around you, as this could fall in a storm and cause severe injury. Termites are one sign of dead wood. Also keep away from coconuts or any other large objects that may fall. Clear away dead and rotting vegetation to make the site less attractive to insects and snakes.

Hammock

A hammock is ideal in tropical regions as it keeps you away from potential flooding and from insects on the ground. Either carry a specialist hammock with mosquito netting or improvise a hammock with a parachute.

A-frame with thatched leaves

Construct an A-type framework and cover it with overlapping layers of banana, atap or other broad leaves.

Platform shelters

These can be made from wood or bamboo lashed together. Bamboo can be split down the sides to create interlocking sections to be used as a bed and/or a roof. Large leaves such as palm and atap can be woven together to create a roof and walls for the shelter as

well as bedding. Take care when handling bamboo, as it can split suddenly when cut and send out sharp splinters. Leaves can be razor sharp and can inflict painful cuts if not handled carefully.

Swamp bed

This should be constructed in such a manner as to keep you out of harm's way in a swamp. Either find four trees in a rectangle or drive four poles into the ground. Then lash some cross poles across at both ends. Poles should then be laid along the long sides, resting on top of the crosswise short poles. Then, place cross bars all the way along the length of the swamp bed, on top of which you can lay leaves and/or grass. Make sure that the bed is large enough for both yourself and your equipment.

Platform shelters

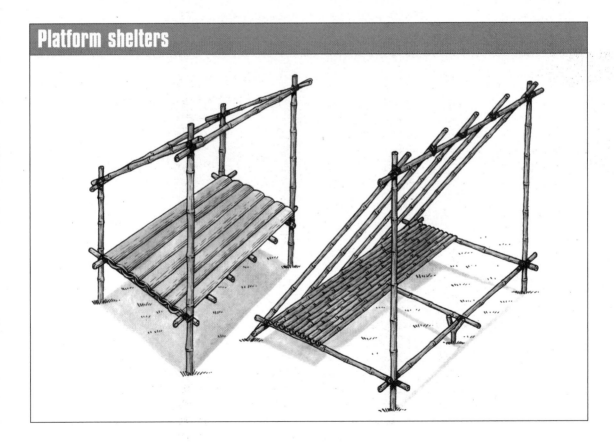

FINDING WATER

Although the tropical survivor is not likely to have the same difficulty as the desert survivor in finding sources of water, the problems should not be underestimated.

To locate water look out for signs of bees, ants or flies, which all need water and may lead you directly to a source. Some birds, such as finches and pigeons, are good indicators of a water source. When they are flying fast and low, they are likely to be heading towards water. When they pause frequently for rest they are likely to be coming away from water.

Sources of water

Streams

If the stream is fast-flowing with a stone and sand bed, the water is likely to be pure, although it is not always possible to ascertain whether there are animal deposits farther upstream. Boil or purify if in doubt.

Rain trap

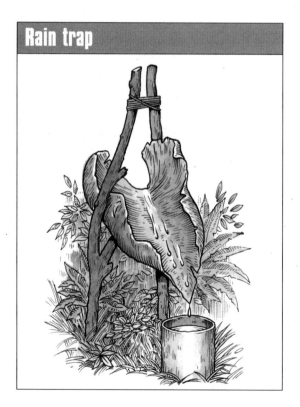

Water purification

The best ways of purifying suspect water are:

- Boil it for at least three minutes.
- Use water-sterilizing tablets.
- Use two or three drops of iodine to 2US pints/1¾UK Pints (1 litre) of water, allowing it to stand for 30 minutes.
- Use a few grains of permanganate of potash (a form of salt derived from permanganic acid) to 2US pints/1¾UK Pints (1 litre) of water and allow it to stand for 30 minutes.

If you are taking water from a stream, don't drink it directly from the surface but use a receptacle so as to check that the water is free from such things as leeches. Muddy water can be strained through a sand-filled cloth or a bamboo pipe filled with leaves and/or grass.

The following sources of water will most probably require purification:

- Stagnant water, such as small pools or water in tree trunks.
- Water holes and large rivers. The water should be strained, allowed to stand for a few hours, strained again, and then purified by boiling or dissolving sterilising tablets.
- Water from digging. You can dig into sand a few yards up from the seashore and stop digging as soon as water starts collecting. This water should be fairly clean and free from salt.

Rain

You can set up a rain trap with large leaves that will funnel rain water into a receptacle.

Bamboo

Sometimes you can find water in the base of large bamboo stems.

Bamboo

Green bamboo
Bend a piece of bamboo and tie it down. Cut off the top and let the water drip into a receptacle over night.

Coconuts
Green, unripe coconuts have a refreshing milk which is a good substitute for fresh water. Do not drink from ripe and fallen coconuts.

Banana or plantain tree stump
Cut the tree, leaving about a 2ft (60cm) stump (A). Scoop out the stump, leaving a bowl-shaped hollow (B). Water will begin to flow into the bowl from the roots.

Vine
Cut a lower portion of vine about four feet in length and catch the liquid that drips out.

Large-leaved plants
In the tropics, plants with large leaves, such as pitcher plants, will catch rainwater. Make

Banana stump

Transpiration bag

Vegetation bag

sure the water is properly strained to extract insects.

Vegetation stills
Tie a translucent plastic bag round a branch so that it covers the foliage at the end. Weigh or tie down the branch so that transpiration water from it can drip into the bag.

Vegetation bag
Place vegetation in a bag and leave it in the sun so that the heat extracts the moisture in the foliage.

Moisture collection
You can tie rags round your ankles and walk through dew-covered grass before sunrise. The rags will become impregnated with water, which you can then wring out into a receptacle. Tie a rag round a slanted tree, leaving one end loose. The water will drip down the rag into a receptacle on the ground.

FINDING FOOD
Food is abundant in the tropics but the usual care should be taken with potentially poisonous plants.

Edible plants
Bael fruit
Found in India and Burma and other tropical rainforests. The fruit grows on a tree about 10–16ft (2.5–5m) tall, and is grey or yellow and contains seeds.

Bamboo
Although native to the Far East, these plants can be found in many parts of the world. The appearance will be familiar and the young shoots, up to about a foot in height, can be eaten raw. The fine black hairs along the edge of the leaves of the young shoot are poisonous and should be removed. You can also eat the bamboo seeds when boiled. Bamboo provides all sorts of uses as shelter frames, water carriers, utensils and tools.

Bamboo

Banana and plantain

Found widely in the humid tropics. These treelike plants have large leaves, and the flowers hang in clusters. You can eat the fruit either raw or cooked. The flowers, rootstocks and leaf sheaths of many species can be boiled and eaten. The centre can also be eaten either cooked or raw.

Banana

Bignay

Found wild, from the Himalayas through Ceylon, South-East Asia and northern Australia. Bignay is a shiny, evergreen shrub with currant-like, red or black fruit. It can be eaten raw or jellied.

Breadfruit

Found in the South Pacific but also the West Indies and Polynesia. A tree with dark green leaves and large, green, round fruit. The fruit can be baked whole on hot embers for about half an hour, or it can be boiled, baked or fried in slices. Its seeds can be boiled or roasted.

Coconut

Found throughout the tropics, mostly near coasts. The white meat inside the fruit can be eaten and the liquid in the unripe fruit is a good thirst-quencher. The palm 'cabbage', or sheath from which the leaves protrude, is found at the top of the plant and may be eaten raw, boiled or roasted.

Coconut

Breadfruit

Fishtail palm

Found in India, Burma, South-East Asia and the Philippines. These tall trees have a large flowering shoot that hangs downwards. The leaves are oval or wedge-shaped, unlike other palms. Juice can be drawn from the palm shoot. The palm cabbage can either be eaten raw or cooked.

Mango

Grown throughout the tropics. The tree has shiny, alternate leaves. The fruit is oval and turns orange when ripe. It is eaten raw.

Manioc

(also known as tapioca or cassava) Widespread in the tropics. The plant is 3–7ft (1–2m) high with large, tuber-like roots. One type of manioc is sweet, the other bitter. The bitter one contains poisonous hydrocyanic acid. Cook the bitter type, grate or mash the roots into pulp, squeeze out the pulp and cook the remaining dough for at least an hour.

Pawpaw

Found in both tropical and some temperate areas. The fruit grows directly from the trunk and tends to turn yellow when ripe. It can be eaten either raw or cooked.

Pawpaw

Rattan palm

Found in rainforests in tropical Africa, Asia, the East Indies and Australia, this is a climber with a whitish flower. Eat the stem tips and palm heart roasted or raw.

Manioc

Edible roots

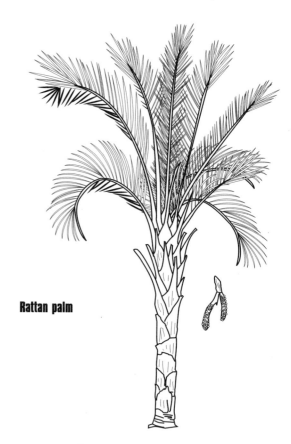

Rattan palm

Nipa palm

Found throughout South-East Asia. The long leaves collect at the base to form what little there is of a trunk. The flower stalk and seeds are a good source of water and food.

Sago palm

Found in South-East Asia, mainly in swamps and by lakes and rivers. The palm is squat with long, arching leaves. The pith of the tree will provide sago, which can be cooked.

Taro

Sugar palm

Sugar palm
Found in many parts of the tropics, with very large leaves. The young flower will yield sugar and the seeds can be boiled.

Sweetsop
Widely distributed in tropical regions, this small tree has a bumpy shaped fruit, which can be eaten raw.

Taro
Found widely in the tropics, this plant is about 2–3ft (0.5–1m) high, and has large heart-shaped leaves. The roots, young leaves and stalks are all edible and should be either boiled or roasted. Change the water when boiling to get rid of any poison.

Water lily
Found in temperate and subtropical regions in streams and lakes. The seeds and thickened roots of any variety of lily may be eaten boiled or roasted.

Water lily

Wild yam

Widely distributed in tropical regions, the yam is a ground creeper, and its root can be boiled and eaten like a vegetable.

Wild yam

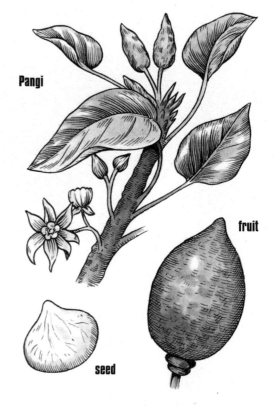

Pangi

Wild rice

Found in wet areas in tropical and temperate climates. It is a tall grass which yields grains which can be collected, threshed and winnowed to remove the husks. The rice can be boiled or roasted and then pounded to make flour.

fruit

seed

Poisonous tropical plants

Castor bean

Deadly poisonous. Native to tropical Africa, it is found in all tropical regions, as well as some temperate regions. It grows to about 40ft (12m) with orange, petalless flowers. The fruit is covered in soft, orange-brown spines. The bean-shaped seeds contain castor oil and are extremely poisonous. All parts of the plant are poisonous.

Cowhage

Dangerously poisonous. Found in the United States and in tropical areas, it has purplish flowers on a vinelike stem, with seeds in brown hairy pods. Skin contact causes irritation, and contact with eyes can cause blindness.

Hemlock

Deadly poisonous. Found worldwide in grassy wastelands. It has hollow purple-spotted stems and dense clusters of small white flowers, white roots and a bad smell.

Castor bean

capsule

female flower

male flower

seeds

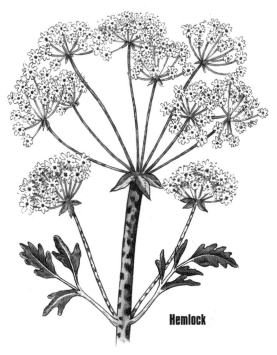

Hemlock

Physic nut

section of fruit

Lantana
Deadly poisonous. Mostly cultivated as an ornamental plant, it can also be found as a weed in tropical and temperate areas. The flowers can be white, yellow, orange, pink or red, with a dark blue, blackberry-shaped fruit. It causes dermatitis.

Manchineel
Dangerously poisonous. Found in the southern United States, Central America and northern South America, this tree can grow to about 50ft (15m) with shiny green leaves and small greenish flowers. The fruit is green to yellow when ripe. It causes dermatitis.

Pangi
Dangerously poisonous. Found in South-East Asia. A tree with heart-shaped leaves and green flowers. It has large, brown, pear-shaped fruit which is particularly poisonous.

Physic nut
Dangerously poisonous. Found in the southern United States and throughout the tropics. A shrub with small green to yellow flowers and apple-sized fruit.

Poison sumas
Dangerously poisonous. Found in swamps in North America. A dark-spotted, smooth-stemmed shrub with green-yellow flowers and white berries. It causes dermatitis.

Rosary pea
Deadly poisonous. Found in Africa, southern North America, the Caribbean and Central and South America. A vine with purple flowers and red and black seeds.

Strychnine tree

Deadly poisonous. Found in South-East Asia and Australia. An evergreen tree that can be 40ft (12m) high. It has greenish flowers and orange to red berries.

Strychnine tree

Section of fruit

Water hemlock or cow bane

Deadly poisonous. Found near water worldwide, including swamps. It has purple-streaked stems, toothed leaflets with clusters of small white flowers, and a solid turnip-like root.

ANIMALS

Animals in the rainforest tend to be small and tree-living, which can make capturing them difficult. The few larger rainforest animals include the elephant and the okapi, a shy and rarely seen relative of the giraffe.

In Africa there are two kinds of pig living in the forest, the bush pig, or red river hog, and the giant forest hog. In Asia, there are three kinds of pig: the common wild boar, the bearded pig and the babirussa, which has upward-growing tusks. In South America, there are two kinds of peccary living in the rainforest, though only the white-tailed peccary is a true tropical rainforest dweller.

All these animals can be dangerous and, realistically, should only be hunted with a rifle or a good spear.

Other animals of the tropical rainforest

Anoa ox (Sulawesi, Indonesia)
Asian water buffalo
Bushbuck (Africa)
Duikers (Africa – incl. Bates' Pygmy
   Antelope, Royal Antelope)
Elephant shrews (Africa)
Forest deer, including sambar, swamp deer,
   axis deer or chital (Asia)
Mouse deer (Asia)
Monkeys and apes
Moon rats (Asia)
Pygmy hippopotamus
Rodents (paca and agouti from South
   America)
Sloths (South America)
Squirrels (Africa and Asia)
Tamarau ox (Philippines)
Tapirs (Asia, South America and Malaysia)
Tree kangaroos (Australia and New Guinea)
Tree shrews (South-East Asia)
Water chevrotain (Africa)
Wild forest ox or gaur (India and Malaysia)

Birds

Birds of paradise (Australia)
Cassowaries (Australia)
Congo peacock (Africa)
Guinea fowl (Africa)
Hornbills (Africa and Asia)
Hummingbirds (South America)
Parrots, including cockatoos, lories and
   pygmy parrots (Australia)
Peacock (India and Sri Lanka)
Pheasants, including jungle fowl (Asia)
Pigeon (including crowned pigeon)
Sunbirds (Africa and Asia)

Turacos (Africa)
Toucans (South America)
Woodcreepers (South America)

Invertebrates
Beetles
Butterflies
Centipedes
Millipedes
Spiders

Predators
Himalayan black bear (Himalaya and Indo-China)
Jaguar (South America)
Leopard (Africa and Asia)
Marsupial tiger cat (Australia)
Small to medium-sized cats
Tiger (Asia)

Reptiles and amphibians
Chameleon (Africa and Asia)
Flattened tree snake (Asia)
Flying frog (Asia)
Flying lizards (Asia)
Gecko (Asia)
Snakes
Tree frogs (Africa, Asia, South America)

Birds, lizards and snakes are all edible, though great care should be taken with the latter. Ants, grubs, grasshoppers and crickets are also edible, though wings and legs should first be removed. Grubs can be split and broiled over a fire.

(See Chapter 10, Trapping, Fishing and Plant Food, for further information.)

POISONOUS SNAKES

Americas
Bushmaster
Deadly poisonous. Found in Central and South America in lowland tropical forests.

Pinkish brown with dark, triangular markings. Length: average 6ft–8ft 6ins (2–2.6m).

Coral snake
Deadly poisonous. Found in southern United States and South America. Distinctly coloured in bands of black, red, yellow and white. Length: average 2ft 3ins (67cm).

Cottonmouth
Dangerously poisonous. Found in southern United States. Coloured brown or olive. Length: average 3ft (90cm).

Eastern diamondback rattlesnake
Dangerously poisonous. Found in the southern United States in swamps and elsewhere. Also capable of swimming out to sea. Olive or brown colour with dark brown or black diamonds. Length: average 5ft (1.5m).

Eyelash pit viper
Deadly poisonous. Found in southern Mexico, Central America and South America. It lives mostly in trees. Its colour can vary from uniform yellow to reddish-yellow spots. Length: average 1ft 6ins (45cm).

Jumping viper
Deadly poisonous. Found in southern Mexico and Central America. Brown or grey with black markings. Length: average 2ft (60cm).

Africa and Asia
Bush viper
Poisonous. Found in most of Africa. It lives mainly in trees but hunts on the ground. Colour varies from pale green through olive to reddish brown. Length: average 1ft 6ins (45cm).

Gaboon viper
Dangerously poisonous. Found in most of Africa, mainly in dense rainforest. The colour varies from pink to brown with yellow or brown spots on the back. Length: average 4ft (1.2m).

Green mamba

Deadly poisonous. Found in most parts of Africa, usually in brush and trees. The green mamba is uniformly coloured, and the larger black mamba is olive or black. Length: 5ft–6ft 6ins (1.5–2m).

Green tree pit viper

Dangerously poisonous. Found in India and South-East Asia. The colour is uniformly bright or dull green. Length: average 1ft 6ins (45cm).

King cobra

Deadly poisonous. Found in South-East Asia and southern China. The colour is green, brown or olive with black bands. Length: average 11ft 6ins (3.5m).

Krait

Deadly poisonous. Found in India and Indonesia. It is coloured in black and white or black and yellow bands. Length: 1–5ft (0.9–1.5m).

Malayan pit viper

Dangerously poisonous. Found in South-East Asia and China. It can be grey, red or fawn, with triangular brown markings outlined by lighter scales, and arrow marks on the head. Length: 2ft–2ft 8ins (60–80cm).

Puff adder

Dangerously poisonous. Found in African savannas and swamps, and Arabian arid regions. Its colour is a yellowy, light brown or orange with chevron-shaped, dark brown or black bars. Length: average 4ft (1.2m); maximum 6ft (1.8m).

Rhinoceros viper or river jack

Dangerously poisonous. Found in equatorial Africa. It has a bright colour with purple to red-brown marks on the back, and is distinguished by scaly horns on its nose. Length: average 2ft 6ins (75cm).

Russell's viper

Deadly poisonous. Found in many areas from India through to Borneo. Its colour is brownish with reddish spots ringed in black in three rows. Length: 3–4ft (1–1.25m).

Wagler's pit viper or temple viper

Dangerously poisonous. Found in Malaysia through to Philippines. Its colour is green with white crossbands edged in blue or purple. Length: average 2ft (60cm).

Australian copperhead

Dangerously poisonous. Found in south Australian and Tasmanian swamps. Its colour is brown, though some are black. Length: average 4ft (1.2m).

DANGEROUS OR UNPLEASANT INSECTS AND SPIDERS

Ants

Red ants nest in the twigs of trees and shrubs and will bite persistently. African termites build nests with overlapping, mushroom-shaped layers on rotting trees, etc.

Centipedes

Found worldwide in damp areas. Mostly harmless but some larger varieties can cause swellings and infections.

Hornets, bees and wasps

These can be found in a variety of forms worldwide. They are best left undisturbed. Stings from several hornets can kill. Wasps tend to attack moving targets, but if a swarm is attacking, run through dense undergrowth.

Leeches

As with ticks, they should not be pulled off. They can be removed in the same way as ticks, or by applying nicotine or raw lime. Carry out regular checks for leeches and brush off those that have not yet got a hold.

Mosquito

Mosquitoes, as many people will know, are deadly. The anopheles mosquito carries malaria and malaria pills provide less than 50 per cent protection against its bite. Always use a mosquito net, if available. If not, improvise with cloth, parachute or large leaves. Particularly at night, tuck trouser legs into socks and shirt sleeves into gloves. Keep a fire smoking at night, and keep away from swampy or stagnant areas, which is where mosquitoes breed.

Scorpions

Dangerously poisonous. They can be found in tropical jungles and are usually darker than the desert varieties. Some jungle varieties can be up to 8ins (20cm) long.

Spiders

Black widow or hourglass

Dangerously poisonous. Found in warm areas worldwide. Small and dark with hourglass markings on the abdomen.

Funnelweb

Deadly poisonous. Found in Australia. Small and black with short legs.

Tarantula

Poisonous, large and hairy. The poison is not as dangerous as their appearance suggests, but it will cause skin irritation.

Ticks

These are common in the tropics and should not be pulled off, since they will leave their jaws embedded in your skin. Heat, petrol or alcohol should make them drop off. If you have caught an animal such as a pig, take care that ticks do not jump off the dead animal on to you.

TRAVEL IN THE JUNGLE

Ideally, to be rescued, you should stay in one place, but the dense jungle canopy will make it difficult for any rescuers in planes or helicopters to locate you. So, although you may be severely restricted by dense vegetation, travel may be the only realistic way of beng found. Owing to the number of obstacles and potential danger from animals, travel in the jungle must be undertaken with great care and planning.

First of all, try to pinpoint your present location. If you land in the jungle by parachute, make a note of rivers and other landmarks before you enter the tree cover. Use your compass to set a course and follow it as closely as possible, bearing in mind that jungle tracks may not be on your course but will be much easier to follow than hacking through dense bush. Take a bearing on a landmark that you can keep in sight, and then choose another one after it, and so on.

If you wish to be able to return to your original location for any reason, mark your trail by leaving cuts in trees or piles of upturned leaves or stones. To find human habitation, you will need to follow the course of a river or stream. Native villages are normally sited on the banks or confluence of rivers. Bear in mind that trails and rivers will often be used by animals at night, many of which will be dangerous.

Dead or decaying vegetation may mean danger from falling branches, so keep clear of it if possible. Steer clear of swamps, as it will be almost impossible to make headway. They are also likely to contain dangerous animals. Never cross a river with a rucksack fully strapped to your back (See Chapter 12, Rafts and River Crossings).

Attention needs to be given regularly to leeches, chiggers and other parasites, which should be cleared from boots, clothing and skin. Also attend to bites or scratches, which quickly turn septic in the jungle. For this reason, shaving, although usually a morale booster in many circumstances, is not a good idea

CHAPTER FIVE

Survival in Polar Regions

Polar survival is dependent on adequate clothing and shelter. With these two elements in place, this environment of low temperatures, wind chill, snow and ice can be mastered like any other.

The north polar region is a frozen ocean, the Arctic Ocean, and the south polar region, or Antarctic continent, is a land mass mostly lying between 10,000 and 13,000ft (3 and 4km) above sea level. This means that it is extremely cold and almost entirely covered by ice which can be up to 10,000ft (3km) thick.

In the polar regions during the winter, the sun can remain below the horizon for several months, so that the only source of warmth is wind flowing in from lower latitudes. In the summer, the sun remains low in the sky, providing little heat, although over the Arctic Circle (66°33'N) the sun is above the horizon 24 hours a day for part of the summer.

The Antarctic continent only supports two species of flowering plant, and the animals in the polar regions are almost entirely dependent on the sea for food. There are almost no land animals in the Antarctic, but the polar bear lives in the Arctic. Birds come into the Arctic in the summer to breed, but they really belong to the tundra regions. Seals can be found in both regions, and penguins are the typical fauna of Antarctica.

PERSONAL CLOTHING

You should have a windproof outer layer which will also be waterproof enough not to absorb melting snow. A breathable fabric is ideal. You should also wear inner layers of insulation.

You should take specialist advice on clothing before entering an extreme cold weather environment. Fortunately, there is a wide variety of newly developed fabrics

Clothing rules

C   Keep it *clean*
O   Avoid *overheating* – ventilate the body
L   Wear *loose* clothing – allowing air to circulate
D   Keep clothing *dry*, both inside and outside

Polar regions

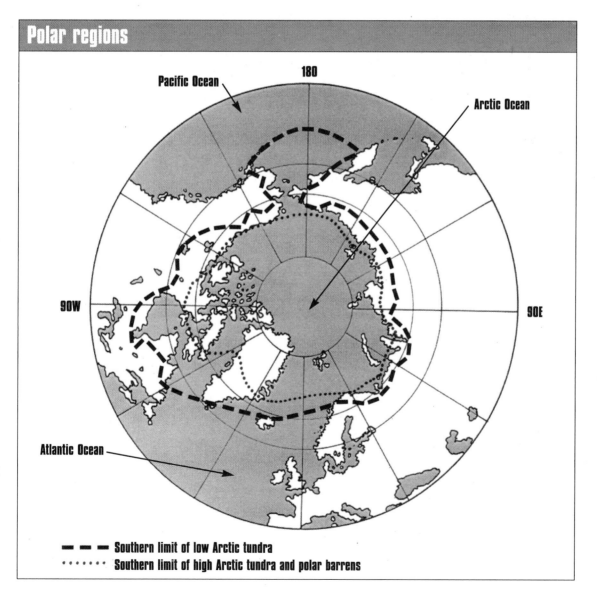

— — — Southern limit of low Arctic tundra
• • • • • • Southern limit of high Arctic tundra and polar barrens

Windchill

Windchill at an air temperature of 32°F (0°C)	
WIND SPEED	WINDCHILL
11mph (5m/s)	16°F (–9°C)
22mph (10m/s)	5°F (–15°C)
34mph (15m/s)	–0.4°F (–18°C)
44mph (20m/s)	–4°F (–20°C)

available, including polypropylene underwear and Gore-Tex outerwear. Use a drawskin hood on your jacket and one which is lined with fur, as this will prevent your breath freezing on your face.

If newer clothing is not available, use wool for the inner layers as it has low water absorbency. Do not wear tight or restrictive clothing, and keep it clean and dry. Loosen or remove items of clothing, such as a hat or gloves, rather than allow yourself to sweat. If you sweat, the clothing will become wet, lose its insulating properties and draw heat away from the body.

If socks and gloves get wet, you can help to dry them out by wrapping them round your stomach. Try to carry as many spare pairs of socks as possible. Dry them over a fire in a shelter if possible.

Waterproof canvas boots known as Mukluks are the ideal footwear. You should wear three layers of socks underneath, which are sized in such a way as to fit over each other.

Fluff out any clothing or bedding that has become compressed – it is the air spaces that are all important in insulation.

Brush off any snow from clothing before entering a shelter or other warm place. Don't get into a sleeping bag with wet clothing. Wear the minimum possible and leave clothes out to air and dry. Fluff out and dry the sleeping bag after use, before rolling it up to protect it.

SHELTER

First of all, get out of the wind. You cannot expect to stay in the open in winter and survive, unless you are moving.

Site of shelter

- In the winter, do not build shelters in the lee of slopes and cliffs where snow may drift heavily and bury your shelter.
- In the summer, do not camp on low-lying ground, which is likely to be damp, or in areas that might flood.
- Choose a place where there will be a cool breeze to keep insects away.
- If you are on sea ice, choose the thickest ice and shelter on the biggest floe. Keep away from thin ice.
- Do not use an aircraft or vehicle as a shelter unless it is well insulated, as the metal conducts heat away.
- A shelter needs to be ventilated, to avoid the risk of carbon monoxide poisoning, especially if a fire is to be constructed inside it.
- The shelter should be large enough to provide room for yourself, companions and equipment, but not so large that it will absorb heat from your bodies. The shelter should be compact and snug.

Natural shelters

Caves and overhanging rockshelves may provide dry shelters. They need to be well insulated in winter, and kept free of insects in summer.

Spruce trees can provide natural shelters in thick snow, if you dig a hole round the base of the tree, the lower branches forming a canopy. Depending on how long you intend to stay, or how effective the lower branches are as cover, you can erect your

Tree well shelter

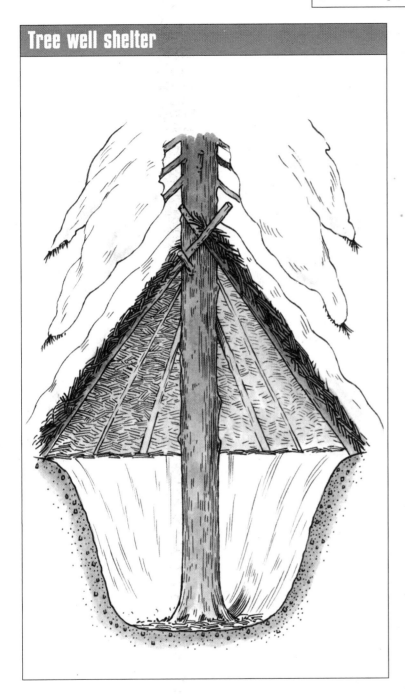

Fallen-tree shelter

Dig out what little snow there is under the tree. If necessary, cut branches from underneath the tree to line the floor.

Snow shelter

Ideal snow to make a shelter is firm enough to take a man's weight without a deeply embedded footprint. Blocks when cut should be about 1ft 6ins (45cm) wide, by 1ft 8ins (50cm) long, and 4–8ins (8–10cm) thick. This will provide insulation and allow light into the shelter.

Snow trench

This allows you to get below the surface, away from wind and snow. You can use snow blocks for overhead cover as well as for a door.

Mark out a rectangle in the snow. Cut out snow blocks just over 4ft (1m) deep from the marked-out area. Cut an L-shaped step 6ins (15cm) deep and 6ins (15cm) wide along the top edges and sides of the trench. Lean two blocks together at the opposite end from the entrance to start forming the roof. Make sure they are offset, i.e. with one of the snowblocks' edges extending beyond the other, so that the next block can be laid in place and supported. Cover

own roof with cut branches and boughs, taking care not to disturb the snow on the tree you will be under. Insulate the hole with branches.

each end with a block and dig a burrow-like hole at one end for an entrance. Alternatively, lay the side blocks upright with roof blocks placed horizontally across.

Igloo or snow house

This requires some skill and practice, and you will also need something like a snow saw or adequate knife to do the job. Draw a circle of about 8–10ft (2.5–3m) diameter in the snow to mark the inside of the igloo. Cut snow blocks from a nearby trench. When you have about 12 blocks you can start building.

Place blocks in a circular row with the side faces of each block angled to the centre of the igloo, and the tops of the blocks sloping inwards. Shave the tops of this row of blocks in a sloping angle to form the first rung of a spiral. Start the next row of blocks, cutting the blocks in such a way as to make the igloo curve inwards. When placing the key block, the hole should be longer than it is wide so that the block can be passed up through the hole and allowed to settle back into position. Pour powdery snow over the structure to seal any gaps. The Inuit sometimes insert a clear sheet of ice as a window.

Inside the igloo cut a subterranean entrance, a sleeping level and a cooking level. You will need insulation on the sleeping level. Place sleeping bags so that the head is nearest the entrance. Use a snow block for the door, which should be left open during the day. Remember to insert ventilation holes.

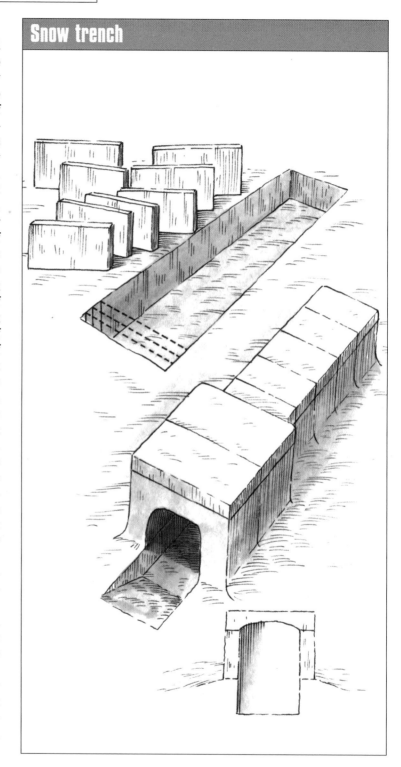

Snow trench

Igloo

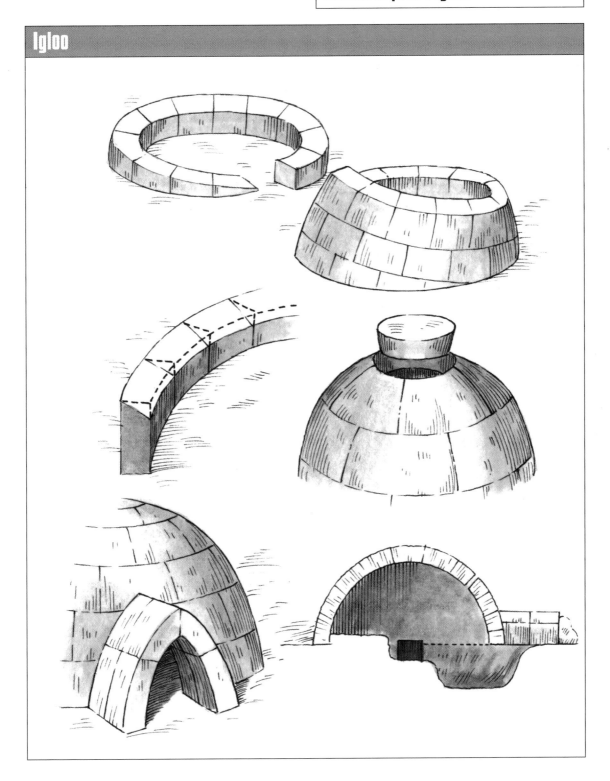

Willow-frame shelter

Inuit igloo

Insert a clear piece of ice or a piece of seal intestine as a window. Have a flap of seal skin near the entrance to help keep the wind out. Cover the bedding area with willow twigs topped with animal furs.

Lean-to shelter

You can sling a horizontal bar between two trees or uprights and lean branches or boughs down the back for shelter, allowing enough space to lie inside with equipment.

You can cover the roof with sod blocks, which should be arranged like tiles to allow water to run off. You can build snow up on the sides where appropriate to provide extra insulation. Build a fire just outside the shelter, with a reflector made of logs or other material to send the heat into the shelter.

Willow-frame shelter

This involves constructing a frame from willows, which can be either upright or elongated. The framework can then be covered with parachute material or with branches, overlaid with sods and snow.

Moulded dome shelter

This shelter requires less expertise and time to construct than, for example, an igloo. Fill a poncho or other large piece of material with bark and small boughs. Cover the material with snow, leaving a gap for the entrance. When the snow has hardened, remove the material and contents, thus creating a living space. Insulate the floor with green boughs and make an entrance block with a smaller amount of material filled with small sticks, etc.

Notes on shelters

- You should always have adequate ventilation, i.e. more than one breathing hole.
- Clearly mark the entrance of the shelter.
- The roof of a shelter should be at least 1ft (30cm) thick.
- Flatten the snow floor well before building the shelter.
- Keep shovels and other tools inside the shelter in case they are needed for digging your way out.

Moulded dome shelter

FIREMAKING

Use any firemaking equipment in your emergency pack, or a stove you may be carrying. To make a fire, you will need to construct the right kind of base and also find kindling and fuel.

Do not build the fire under a snow-covered tree or near anything that is likely to put it out. The fire should be constructed on a firm platform which you can make out of green wood logs, or stones. Failing that, you can dig down to firm soil. If you want to cook, construct a frame to concentrate the heat and to hang a pot on. If you want to heat a shelter, construct a reflector.

Fuel

Pick up kindling during the day wherever you can find it. Dead trees are best for fuel, though birch will burn if split, and green wood will burn on a hot fire. Cassiope is a plant used by Eskimos for fuel when there is no other wood. Other fuels can be peat, animal dung and dry grass twisted together.

Lighting the fire

Make sure everything is easily to hand before attempting to light the fire. If you have matches, use one to light a candle or a bundle of sticks with which you can then light the fire. When kindling is lit, gradually add the fuel, without packing it too densely. Blow on the fire if necessary.

(See Chapter 9, Firemaking, Tools and Weapons, for further information on making fires.)

COLD CLIMATE AILMENTS

Dehydration

Layers of clothing can mean that you will sweat and become dehydrated.

Symptoms

Urine is a thick yellow colour, and a headache is developing.

Treatment

Ensure that you drink enough water to restore the balance. You should know that you are all right, and that the water has filled your cells, when your urine is clearer and your head feels clearer too. Allowing yourself to become dehydrated will affect your ability to think and plan.

Prevention

Make sure you drink an adequate amount of water every day, and do not allow yourself to sweat excessively. Adjust your clothing accordingly.

Hypothermia

This means that the body temperature is below normal.

Symptoms

Lowered resistance to cold, excessive shivering and sluggish movement and thinking.

Treatment

Return the body to normal temperature as soon as possible. Ideally this should be by immersion of only the torso in warm water (100° to 110°F/37.7° to 43.3°C). Care should be taken with this treatment, as total immersion in warm water could result in shock and cardiac arrest.

In a survival environment, the most likely cure is to wrap the patient in a sleeping bag with someone who is warm. Ideally, both should be naked. Do not delay too long, and if the person is conscious start to give him/her hot, sweetened fluids.

It is not enough simply to remove the patient from the source of heat after the body temperature has returned to normal, as the patient is apt to revert to a low temperature once he/she is removed from the source of heat. Allow the patient to regain a reserve of body heat by keeping him/her warm and administering hot drinks as necessary.

Prevention

Do not allow yourself or others to undergo continuous periods of cold without food, hot drinks or other sources of warmth, and beware the danger of getting wet, especially in a wind.

If you fall into water in polar regions:
- Swim violently and rapidly to land.
- Roll yourself in snow, which will absorb some of the water.
- Get yourself to a shelter and warmth as fast as possible.
- Brush off loose snow before entering the shelter.
- Dry your clothing and take hot drinks and food.

Frostbite
Symptoms
This is a serious injury to the skin and sometimes other body tissues by freezing or by formation of ice crystals in the tissue cells. It usually occurs when the temperature is below 10°F (12°C) but can occur at around 32°F (0°C) when there is a windchill factor or when the patient has got wet. Since the cold has an anaesthetic effect, frostbite may not be immediately noticed by the victim.

Frostbite normally affects those parts of the body that have the least protection, such as the face, nose, ears, hands and feet. The first signs are a dull whitish colour in the skin, then the formation of blisters, followed by the death of some skin cells and underlying tissue.

Treatment
- Warm up the affected area and ensure it does not freeze again.
- Put affected hands inside clothing near the body.
- Place frostbitten feet inside a companion's clothing.
- Do not burst blisters but dust them with antiseptic powder.

- Cover the affected area with surgical dressing or some other clean material.
- Do not dip the affected area into hot water or try to warm by a fire. Use body warmth instead.
- Use morphia if there is much pain.
- Serious and deep cases of frostbite should be treated by trained medical personnel.

Prevention
- Do not wear tight clothing, which reduces circulation and increases the risk of frostbite.
- Keep out of the wind as far as possible.
- Do not go outside without adequate clothing.
- Keep clothing dry.
- Move extremities as far as possible, including the face by making expressions and exercising the facial muscles.
- Do not touch cold metal with bare hands.
- Take special care if you are tired and low in energy.
- Do not allow yourself to be splashed with gas (petrol) on bare flesh.

Trench foot
Symptoms
Long exposure to cold and wet can cause feet to turn pale, numb, cold and stiff. The feet will begin to swell, making walking painful. If allowed to continue, this condition can be serious, so make sure feet and footwear are dried as soon as possible.

Treatment
Handle feet with care – do not rub or massage. Clean with soap and water, dry the feet and then keep them raised. Do not walk if you are suffering from this condition. Put on dry socks and make sure there is always a spare, dry pair available.

Prevention
Keep footwear as dry as possible and change socks frequently.

Snow blindness

This is caused by the intense glare of the sun, which is reflected off the snow or intensified by ice crystals in clouds.

Symptoms

Sensitivity to glare. Pinkish vision and watering eyes. Intensifying of reddening vision and pain like grit in the eyes. Loss of vision behind painful, red curtain and sharp pain.

Treatment

Urgently place bandage over the eyes and/or place the patient in a dark place. A cool, wet bandage may help relieve the pain. Time is required for the eyes to recover.

Prevention

Wear sunglasses. If sunglasses are not available, improvise eye shades by cutting slits in bark or some other material and placing them over the eyes. Rubbing charcoal into the skin around the eyes will help to reduce glare.

Carbon monoxide poisoning

This is particularly dangerous in extreme cold climates because shelters are likely to be small and well sealed against the elements, increasing the risk of insufficient ventilation. Carbon monoxide, whicht is both colourless and odourless, will be given off by any gas or stove.

Symptoms

These are difficult to detect, especially when they are happening to yourself, but will include slight headache, dizziness, drowsiness, nausea and maybe vomiting; the patient may also suddenly fall unconscious.

Treatment

- Remove the patient to fresh air or a well-ventilated area and get him/her to breathe deeply.
- If unconscious, apply artificial respiration in a well-ventilated area.

- Give oxygen if available.
- When recovered, the patient should be allowed to rest and be given warm drinks.
- The patient should not undertake heavy work until fully recovered.

Prevention

Keep all shelters well ventilated, which means having at least two ventilation holes to allow circulation. Do not let fires burn up too high. Turn off all stoves and lamps before going to sleep.

FINDING WATER

There is no lack of water in polar regions, but the quantity of water obtained from snow and ice will depend on the amount of fuel available to melt it. It is preferable to melt ice rather than snow, as the volume of water will be greater. You should not sacrifice water intake to save fuel as this will eventually lead to serious side-effects. Limit the amount of water lost through sweat by loosening or removing clothing when working.

In the summer, water can be obtained from streams, lakes and ponds. In tundra regions the water may be stained brown by vegetation, but it is still fit to drink. Despite the fact that water in polar regions is, comparatively, cleaner than in other regions of the world, you should still purify water before you drink it and, if necessary, strain it.

In winter you can obtain water most easily from lakes under the ice and snow. Since the lower surface of the ice follows the contours of the surface of the snow above it, you should dig where the snow is deepest and then chip through the ice under this to find the least cold water.

When heating snow, melt a little at a time and wait until it is fully melted before adding more. Otherwise, the unmelted snow will draw up the water and the pot will burn.

Old sea ice yields much better drinking

water than young ice, which will still be salty. Old sea ice will be rounded and have a bluish tinge.

Do not fill your water bottle right to the top with water – you need to allow some movement in the water to prevent it freezing again. Also, keep the water bottle close to your body.

FINDING FOOD

Ideally, you should have at least two hot meals a day in an extremely cold environment, as well as an occasional hot drink. Food is not abundant in polar regions, though in summer months you should easily be able to obtain fish and other water life from coastal waters, streams, rivers and lakes. You should easily be able to find clams, crawfish, mussels, snails, limpets, chitons, sea urchins and King Crab on most Arctic shores. Do not eat dead shellfish. The small black-purple mussel of the northern Pacific waters is poisonous and should be avoided.

Do not eat fish that have sunken eyes, slimy gills, flabby flesh or skin, or an unpleasant smell. Do not eat any kind of jellyfish. Kelp and other smaller seaweed are edible, though you should avoid seaweed that has long filaments and tendrils.

Ice fishing

Ice may be as much as 12 feet (4m) thick, so you will need to choose an appropriate spot to create a borehole for fishing, where the ice is not too thick to make a hole but thick enough to bear your weight. You can dangle a line on the end of a small stick with some form of signalling device attached to it, such as a handkerchief or piece of card. Tie this stick to another which is across the fishing hole. When a fish bites it should cause the pennant to spring up. (see Chapter 10, Trapping, Fishing and Plant Food, for further advice on fishing techniques.)

LAND ANIMALS

Polar bears are normally found near the coast and should be treated with extreme caution. Only tackle one if you have a good rifle as they are very dangerous animals.

In spring, earless seals can be found basking on the ice near their breathing holes. They are extremely vigilant, however, and difficult to approach. You are only likely to be able to kill a seal with a clear shot to the brain, and preferably before it slides into the water, as it will be very difficult to retrieve.

Take care that you are not stalked by a polar bear, which may be able to smell the blood of a newly killed seal.

ANIMALS OF THE TUNDRA

Tundra is the name for large areas of northern Asia and Canada covered by treeless vegetation.

Arctic hares

These animals forage throughout the winter.

Caribou

Lives in the far north of Canada and makes distant migrations.

Lemming

The most common small herbivore of the tundra. Lemmings migrate, and many famously meet their end when trying to negotiate water barriers.

Musk-ox

Does not migrate but braves the winter within the Arctic circle.

Reindeer

Eurasian equivalent of the Caribou; migrates south each winter.

Predators
Arctic fox

Another common predator, which, like the stoat, turns white in winter.

Arctic fox

Ptarmigan
Remains in the Arctic all year round. Hens dig shallow burrows in open ground, in which they lay 8–13 eggs.

Sea duck (including eiders)
Dive to the bottom to find food.

Snowy owl
Preys on ptarmigan and grouse.

Swan
Also breed in summer.

Terns
The Arctic tern breeds in southern parts of the Arctic and winters in the Antarctic.

Waders
Shorebirds that search for food in shallow waters.

Willow grouse
Also remains in the Arctic.

Stoat
Prey on lemmings and their numbers rise and fall accordingly.

Wolf
Preys on the caribou and follows its path of migration.

Birds
Auks
These are deep divers that feed on fish.

Goose
Common in the Arctic area, where they breed in the summer.

Gyr falcon
Also preys on ptarmigan and grouse.

Gulls
Sometimes rest inland.

Ptarmigan

ANIMALS OF THE TAIGA

Taiga is the name for northern forest that merges into the tundra region in the north and into deciduous forest or grassland in the south. The Taiga extends from north-eastern Europe across Russia to the Pacific Ocean, and across North America from Alaska to Newfoundland. Much of the taiga is north of the Arctic circle and, although its winters may be just as cold as tundra regions, the summers tend to be warmer.

Moose
The largest deer in the world. Eurasian version is the elk.

Shrews
Remain active throughout the winter.

Squirrels
Remain active throughout the winter.

Tree porcupine
Found in North America, and also remains for the winter.

Voles
Red-backed voles live in burrows; climb well.

Wood lemming
Hibernates during the winter.

Predators
Large stoat or ermine
Turns white in winter.

Lynx
Nocturnal predator approximately 31–39ins (80–100cm) long.

Martens
These weasel-like carnivores are also capable of climbing well

Weasels
Medium brown above, white or cream below. Northern species (stoats) molt into white in winter.

Birds
Eurasian capercaillie
The capercaillie is the largest of the grouse family.

Woodpeckers
The northern three-toe woodpecker ranges across the subarctic Northern hemisphere.

Shrew

PLANTS

The following plants grow in arctic and sub-arctic regions, though keep in mind that almost all plants found in these regions are smaller than those found in more temperate zones. Some of the larger black lichens are edible, and are known as rock tripe. They have been used for food by starving explorers.

Tundra vegetation has few species that are edible. The Eskimos eat the black crowberry either raw or mixed with animal oil. Europeans sometimes eat the cloudberry, bilberry and mountain cranberry. Some mushrooms are edible.

Look out for where animals and particularly birds are feeding, as this will lead you to vegetation. Also, when walking, pick up any edible vegetation you see so that you gradually accumulate enough for a meal.

Arctic willow
Found in tundra regions of North America, Europe and Asia. Forms in mats with rounded leaves and yellow catkins. It is high in vitamin C and you can eat raw the inner portion of the new shoots as well as the young roots. Both need peeling.

Bearberry
Found in Arctic and temperate regions. Forms matts with club-shaped leaves and pink or white flowers. The red berries can be eaten raw or cooked and you can make tea from its leaves.

Crowberry
Found in tundra regions of North America and Eurasia. A small shrub with needlelike, evergreen leaves. It has small, black berries, which can be eaten raw or dried for later use.

Fireweed
Found in wood and beside streams and seashores in Arctic regions. Tall with pink flowers and fine leaves. The leaves, stems and flowers are edible but best in spring before the plant becomes tough.

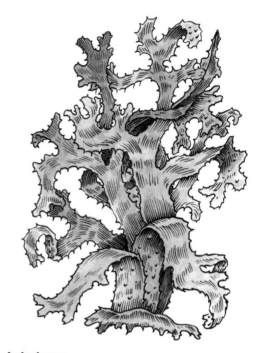

Iceland moss

Iceland moss
Found exclusively in the Arctic in open areas. Can be a variety of grey-green, white or brownish red. All parts are edible but should be soaked, then thoroughly boiled.

Marsh marigold
Found in the Arctic and subarctic regions in bogs, lakes and some streams. Rounded, dark green leaves on a short stem and yellow flowers. All of the plant is edible but should be boiled.

Crowberry

Reindeer moss

Found in open, dry areas. It has hollow, grey stems and antler-like branches. All of the plant is edible but should be soaked for several hours before boiling thoroughly.

Rock tripe

Can be found on stones and boulders. It has a rounded appearance with curling edges. Top of the plant normally black, underside lighter. All of the plant is edible though it can be an irritant if eaten raw. Soak for a lengthy period, change water and boil well; roast as well to make it crunchy.

Rock tripe

Spatterdock or yellow water lily

Found in shallow calm water. Has yellow flowers which develop into bottle-shaped fruits. All of the plant is edible. Seeds can be roasted and ground for flour. The root can be boiled.

TRAVEL

The decision to travel when in a survival predicament should be based on the likelihood of reaching safety as opposed to rescuers being able to find you, especially if you are near a large object like a crash-landed plane.

Other factors include the weather and your own physical condition. You should not venture out in a blizzard or, if a blizzard is threatening, you need to be fully aware that travel will involve plenty of physical exertion and an increased amount of food and water. You will also need to be able to build temporary shelters en route.

When crossing thin ice, lie flat and crawl so as to distribute your weight. The Arctic air is very clear, which makes it difficult to estimate distances, as in deserts. You are in danger of underestimating distances since objects appear closer than they actually are. Make camp early to allow adequate time to build a shelter. Use snow shoes if the snow is deep. These can be made out of willow.

You will need to be able to determine your present position as well as your intended route. There are some signs that will help you:

Stars

In the northern hemisphere, true north can be gauged from the constellation of Ursa Major (Great Bear), which points to the North Star, standing over the North Pole. In the southern hemisphere the southern cross indicates the direction of south. You cannot estimate your latitude from the North Star's height over the horizon to any degree of accuracy without a sextant and a set of tables.

Sun

If you have the correct local time, the shadow cast by a straight object perpendicular to the ground at midday will indicate north and south.

Sky map

Clouds over snowless ground or water will appear black, while clouds over snow or sea ice will be white. Pack ice and drifted snow will create a mottled effect in the clouds.

Birds

Sea birds generally fly out to sea in the morning and return to land in the afternoon.

Flora

Moss will be thickest on the north side of rocks or trees. Alder bark is lighter on the south side. Lichens are more numerous on the south side.

CHAPTER SIX

Survival in Mountains

Mountains offer little protection from low temperatures and high winds. The first rule of mountain survival, therefore, is to find a way of descending as safely as possible.

Mountains are largely inhospitable areas in which to be caught unprepared. Mountain climbing is a specialist skill beyond the scope of this book, but what follows are some of the basic skills which will help you survive and reach safety in mountainous regions.

Mountains usually exist in ranges which consist of peaks, ridges and intermontane valleys. Although some mountains stand on their own, the smallest group is usually the range which can be made up of either a single ridge or a series of ridges. Closely related ridges are called mountain systems, and more than one system joined together is called a mountain chain. A mixture of ranges, systems and chains is called a belt or cordillera.

CLIMATE

Temperature falls at a more or less constant rate with increasing altitude – about 33–34°F (0.5–1°C) for every 328ft (100m). Wind systems are forced by mountains to rise and cool as they do so, causing higher precipitation on windward mountain slopes. When

Mountain lands

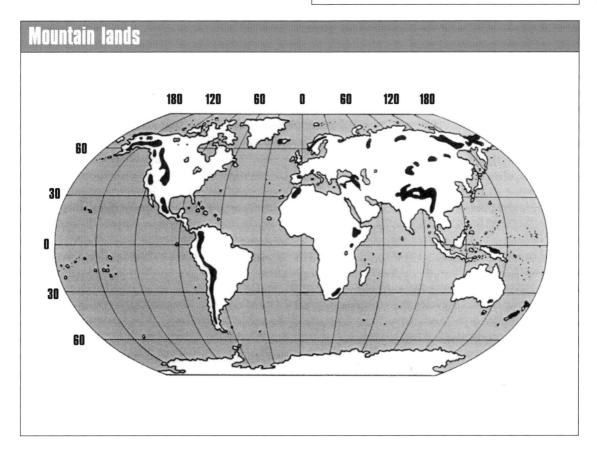

the wind descends the leeward slope, it warms up and precipitation reduces, creating rain shadow.

Mountains in desert regions receive little rain because the air is so dry. On equatorial mountains, although temperatures are low at high altitudes, winter and summer are indistinguishable. There are rapid changes in temperatures, from about 28°F to 46°F (-2°C to 8°C).

Mountains in temperate regions have strongly marked seasons, being sometimes frost-free even at night in the summer, but with temperatures often below freezing in the winter.

There are also microclimate variations. Mountain sides facing the equator in temperate regions are significantly warmer than those on the opposite side.

Typically, ascending a mountain in a temperate region will involve passage through deciduous broad-leaved trees, then evergreen coniferous forest and then, after what is called the timberline – the area above which photosynthesis is not enough to allow trees to grow – an area of tundra-like dwarf shrubs and herbs is reached. After that, vegetation can be almost non-existent.

PERSONAL CLOTHING AND EQUIPMENT

Depending on how high you are up a mountain, you will either be cold or very cold. Having the right kind of clothing will make a big difference.

Layers

The layering system is not new; it is simply

Significant mountains of the world

ASIA	FEET	METRES
Everest (China-Nepal)	29,028	8848
K2 (Kashmir-Sinkiang)	28,250	8611
Nanda Devi (India)	25,643	7816
Ararat (Turkey)	16,808	5123
Jaya (Indonesia)	16,503	5030
Kinabalu (Malaysia)	13,431	4094
Fuji (Japan)	12,388	3776
NORTH & CENTRAL AMERICA		
McKinley (USA)	20,320	6194
Logan (Canada)	19,551	5959
Citlaltepetl (Mexico)	14,688	4477
SOUTH AMERICA		
Aconcagua (Argentina)	22,834	6960
Huascaran (Peru)	22,205	6768
Sajama(Bolivia)	21,463	6542
Chimborazo (Ecuador)	20,702	6310
EUROPE		
El'brus (Russian Federation)	18,510	5642
Mont Blanc (France-Italy)	15,744	4808
Matterhorn (Italy-Switzerland)	14,688	4477
Etna (Sicily)	10,902	3323
AFRICA		
Kilimanjaro (Tanzania)	19,340	5895
Kirinyaga (Kenya)	17,057	5199
Stanley (Zaire)	16,763	5110
Toubkal (Morocco)	13,664	4165
AUSTRALASIA		
Cook (New Zealand)	12,316	3754
ANTARCTICA		
Vinson Massif	16,066	4897
Erebus	12,447	3794

the case that the range of materials has substantially improved. Whereas early climbers were restricted to variations on wool and tweed, climbers today have a wide range of synthetic fibres from which to choose, most of which are available from local department stores.

Base layer

The idea of this is that a thin layer of, usually, synthetic material should transfer moisture from the skin away from the body, while being too thin to absorb moisture that may be coming in from outside. The result is that you should always remain reasonably dry despite the level of exertion or outside conditions.

Insulating layer

The latest and most effective insulating material is fleece, which has developed from being the preserve of the cognoscenti to a ubiquitous fashion item. It is worth taking care when choosing a fleece, as there are different thicknesses and some have breathable material inserted. There are other factors to consider, such as ventilation zippers and stretch fleeces.

As in most cases, apart from rainforest wear, thin trousers are ideal for walking since they allow ease of movement and dry easily. Obviously, warmer overtrousers, such as Mountain

Equipment Ultrafleece, should be worn in extreme cold.

Shell layer
Ideally this should be a breathable fabric such as Gore-Tex. For mountains, a three-ply layer is recommended. Other variations can be considered, such as Patagonia H2NO. If you are mountaineering, you will want to ensure that the clothing you buy is adaptable to the activity and to the extra equipment you may be wearing, such as a helmet. Overtrousers should be designed in such a way – perhaps with articulated knees – as to allow ease of movement, .

Single-layer system
This is a cheaper option, perhaps for those who do not wish to invest so much time and money in a particular outdoor activity. The emphasis is on breathability and the transfer of moisture away from the body.

All the above garments will function much better if they are kept clean and properly maintained.

Boots
There is a huge variety of boots available on the market, most of which are good. It is important to remember, however, that boots are built in different ways according to the type of conditions or environment that they are to be used in and should be selected with care. Obtain specialist advice on boots from an expert in a reputable, outdoor equipment shop (but always bear in mind that the salesman's job is to sell you something). Do your own research through magazines, which sometimes carry special equipment surveys.

The major grades of conditions for which you will require different boots are hillwalking, winter mountaineering and snow and ice-climbing. Boots that are flexible and ideal for hillwalking will not provide the stiffness and support required to negotiate snow without crampons. If you are planning to do winter or Alpine walking, therefore, wear stiff-soled boots with supportive uppers. Crampons can be added when necessary, and will be more effective on this kind of boot.

Ice axe
To move on snow and ice, this is a basic piece of equipment that can be used for support, braking, digging and probing. Its basic components are the head (adze and pick), a shaft and a spike.

Ski stick
This will make movement through snow easier. You can carry a telescopic ski stick in a backpack.

MOUNTAIN HAZARDS

Avalanche
While an avalanche can occur wherever snow lies but it is influenced by certain conditions. If the snow is well bound together, then the risk of avalanche is reduced. If there are marked differences in the hardness of layers of snow, then the risk of avalanche increases.

You can assess the likelihood of an avalanche by digging into the snow in a representative area to test the hardness. If you prod the snow with an axe shaft and notice sudden changes in resistance, that is quite a good sign that the area is prone to avalanche. You can perform the test more thoroughly by digging a snow profile, preferably all the way to the ground, which will allow you to assess differences in hardness, moisture content and crystal size in the various layers of snow.

Water is a lubricant, so if the snow is very wet it will be denser and heavier, and more likely to slide. A rough guide to the wetness of snow is that if you can make a snowball out of the snow, it is quite wet. If your gloves are dripping wet from handling the snow, it is very wet.

Ground

If the ground is hard and smooth, then snow is more likely to slide over it. Long grass will also provide a slippery surface for snow.

Slope

If the slope is concave, it is less likely to have an avalanche. If it is convex, it is more likely to have an avalanche. Obviously, the angle of the slope is also an important factor. The steeper the slope, the more likely the snow is to slide off it. Slopes of between 20° and 50° are most likely to have an avalanche.

Wind slab

The most common type of avalanche is called wind slab, and is caused by the effect of wind on falling or fallen snow. Wind slab snow is chalky in appearance, has a fine texture and makes a squeaky noise when walked on.

Powder snow

Avalanches can be caused when powdery snow accumulates in conditions of no or little wind. Over 1ft 4ins (40cm) of fresh snow is an indicator of a high risk of this kind of avalanche.

Ice

Avalanches caused by ice usually occur in warm weather when ice masses fall after thawing. Pinnacles of ice, or seracs, are most likely to fall in the morning or evening, due to the change in temperature.

Wet snow

A rapid rise in temperature or an area exposed to direct sunlight implies the risk of a wet snow avalanche. See if there are snowballs running down a hill, which is an indicator of this kind of avalanche.

What to do in areas at risk of avalanche

- Cross a danger zone one at a time, connected by a rope.
- Cross the slope as high as possible.
- Take advantage of any available protection, such as rock outcrops.
- If you are caught in an avalanche, do your best to maintain your present position. This may mean digging your axe into an area of snow above you that is not moving. By staying where you are, you will allow the dangerous snow to pass safely below you.
- If you are falling in an avalanche, try to move across to the side of the fall by rolling sideways. Use swimming motions to try to remain near the surface. If still caught in the avalanche when it has stopped, use all your energy to 'swim' to the surface.
- If you are buried, try to clear a breathing space in front of the face.
- Conserve oxygen by not shouting, which is unlikely to be heard anyway.

Rescue

If you see someone taken by an avalanche:
- Mark the spot where you saw him/her before the avalanche fell, and then the place where the avalanche hit the person. Follow the line through these two points and continue it below to find the most likely place of burial.
- Call for help, but do not leave the area to find assistance that is more than 15 minutes away.
- Look for anything like personal items that may indicate where the burial site is.
- Systematically check the area by probing with an axe shaft or other means.
- On finding the victim, clear the mouth and airways. Remove the weight of snow from the chest. Give artificial respiration immediately if the person is not breathing, even before fully removing the body from the snow.

Avalanche risk

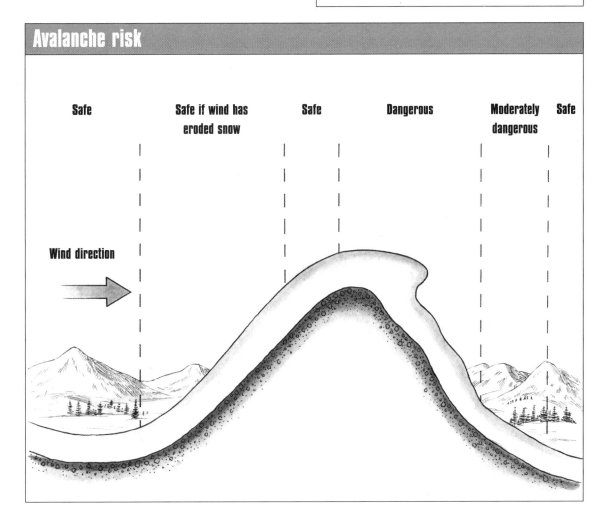

Safe	Safe if wind has eroded snow	Safe	Dangerous	Moderately dangerous	Safe

Wind direction

Cornice

These are overhanging masses of snow which usually form on the crests of ridges and plateaus, but which can occur at any sharp changes of angle. The most common angle of slope on which a cornice forms is 17°.

A cornice can break off well back from the actual edge, so keep as far away from the edge as possible. It is advisable to be roped up when you are negotiating a ridge with a cornice.

Glacier

A glacier is a mass of ice in an area of permanent snow. The weight of snow creates a pressure that turns snow to ice, which then begins to move downhill under the force of gravity. As the glacier moves, it melts, and only stops moving when the amount that has melted is equivalent to the accumulation of snow at the source of the glacier.

The surface of the glacier is a brittle crust which can crack under the strains of glacial movement to form features such as crevasses, ice falls, seracs, etc., all of which constitute dangers for mountaineers.

The glacier picks up crushed rock, which is known as moraine. The rock may then be deposited in ridges along the side (lateral moraine), along the centre (medial moraine)

Rescue search

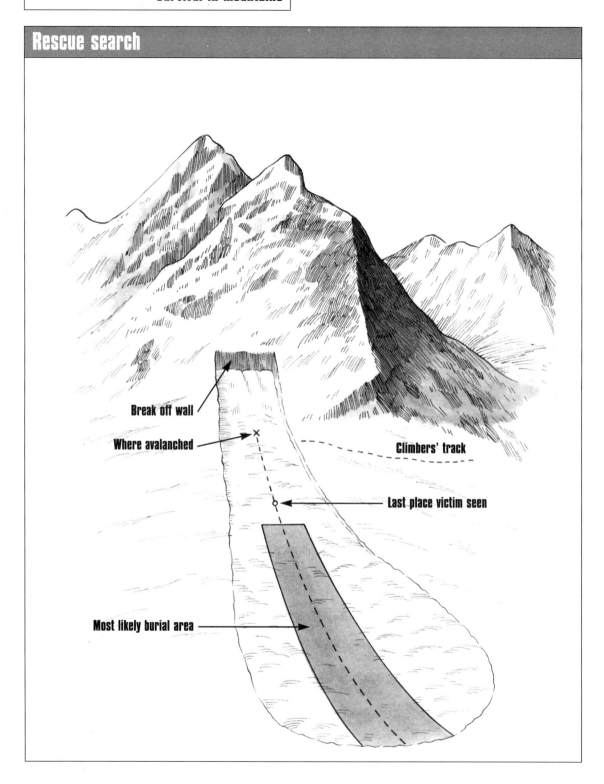

Break off wall

Where avalanched

Climbers' track

Last place victim seen

Most likely burial area

and at the end of the glacier (terminal moraine). Moraines can be loose and dangerous to traverse.

Moving on glaciers

- Take special care in areas where the glacier starts to become steeper or where it bends, as this will create dangerous features.
- Take care with snow bridges (which cross crevasses) as they might give way at any moment.
- Try to cross a glacier in the early morning when it is still cold, before ice has turned to meltwater.
- If the glacier is covered with fresh snow, features like crevasses will be difficult to see and, therefore, climbers should be roped up to each other. It is much safer to be roped up whatever the conditions.
- Temperatures may be high on the glacier during the day, but climbers should take care about how much clothing they remove because, if they fall into a crevasse, the temperature will plummet.

When roped up, allow about 82ft (25m) of rope between at least two, and preferably three or more, people. Some rope can be coiled round the body, over the right shoulder and under the left

Diagonal ascent

arm, to make a distance between walkers of about 50ft (15m). An overhand knot should be tied round the coils and the main rope. Loose coils of rope should never be carried, and the rope should never be slack between the climbers. If the first man falls into a crevasse, the rest of the team should quickly move backwards and down on their haunches, with their heels dug into the snow to stop the fall.

Approach a crevasse at right angles, and if jumping one remember that snow may be loose on the far side. Make sure you fall for-ward after the jump, preferably with an ice axe to dig in at the other side. Keep an eye out for any abnormalities in the surface of the snow, such as dark patches or dips, which may be covering a crevasse.

MOVING IN MOUNTAIN SNOW AND ICE

You can kick steps when walking in snow, but on ice wear crampons (on the correct kind of stiff boots).

Direct ascent

Hold the ice axe with the pick pointing

Braking positions

Braking without an axe

backwards and use it for support. Only move it when both feet are fully secure in steps. Kick a step into the snow, which is angled slightly downwards. The step should be deep enough to take at least half the foot, though this may not be possible in very hard ground.

Diagonal ascent

The steps should be horizontal, created with the side of the boot, and angled slightly into the hill. Kick along the slope to saw away the snow. Push the axe into the hill with the inside hand for stability and security.

Descent

This time the steps are made with the heel of the boot, with an almost stiff leg.

Arresting a fall

If you slip and you have an ice axe, immediately drive the shaft vertically into the slope and keep one hand holding it near the base. Kick both toes into the snow to get a foothold. On harder snow, the pick of the ice axe should be used, forcing it into the snow to create a brake.

Braking position

One hand should be on the head of the axe and the other on the shaft. If the left hand is on the axe head, the adze should be under the left shoulder, with the right hand on the shaft to the side of the body. The pick should be forced into the slope by pushing down with the right arm and shoulder. The adze of the axe should be pushed into the hollow just below the collar bone. Pressure should be on the axe and on the knees with feet raised.

The above is the basic position, but obviously you may not be in the ideal position when you fall. The important thing is to act as quickly and instinctively as possible. Practice with the guidance of a good climbing manual will make a big difference.

Braking without an axe

If you lose the axe in a fall or do not have one, use your arms, feet, hands and legs to break the fall. One technique is to roll on your front, push up from the slope with your arms and concentrate all the pressure on your toes. This has a wedge effect which should bring you to a halt.

Glissading

If you intend to glissade, you should be competent at ice-axe braking. Only glissade if you can see where you will stop.

Standing glissade

Like skiing, you should adopt a relaxed position with knees slightly bent and the feet apart. Hold out the arms for balance. Turn by moving the body, and stop by turning the feet across the slope.

Crouching glissade

Crouch down grasping the ice axe, with one hand on the top and the other on the shaft. Drag the spike of the axe in the snow for balance. To brake, put your weight on the shaft of the axe.

Sitting glissade

Sit on the snow and slide down, using the axe in the same way as in the crouching glissade. If you lie back and raise your feet, you will go faster. To stop, put your feet down and use the axe.

DESCENDING FROM A HILL OR MOUNTAIN

Descent is your main priority, because on a mountain you will be both cold and exposed. If you need to rest and find temporary shelter, work your way round to the lee of the mountain, out of the wind.

- Look out for worn paths or other signs that the route has been used by people, to make your descent easier.
- In poor visibility, you will need to be

Abseiling 1

Abseiling 2

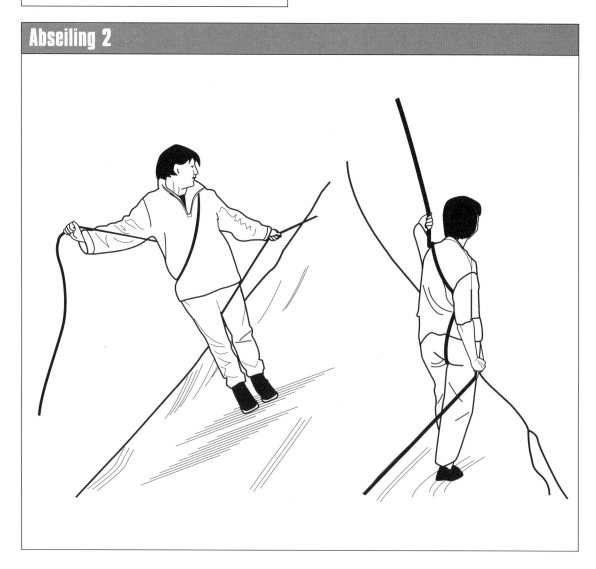

extremely cautious, as finding your way in a mist is difficult even for experienced climbers with compasses.

- If you are scrambling down a hillside, make sure you are facing inwards towards the rock.
- Avoid gullies, as the risk of stone falls is greater. If you are in a group, ensure that those below are not in danger of being hit by rocks loosened by those above.
- You should not have to use a rope on a hill; however it is always wise to carry a rope in case of real emergencies.
- If traversing a glacier in a group, keep roped together. Follow existing tracks if possible, but be aware that they may have been left by inexperienced climbers.
- Beware of slopes covered with small, loose stones (scree), as they may lead to a cliff which you cannot see from the top.

Abseiling

The following description of a classic abseil assumes you are only equipped with a rope.

Belaying

Abseiling is not an easy option and is treated with caution by even the most experienced climbers. Pictures of civilians abseiling off buildings may give a false impression – they are usually under strict guidance by experienced servicemen who also act as anchor men. Resort to abseiling only if there are no options, or if you or a companion are trained in the technique.

How to abseil

First of all find a solid anchor; a second anchor point may be used as a backup. The anchor should ideally be located above the ledge on which you are standing. Make sure the rope will not move once it is under strain. Keep the rope clear of narrow cracks, which may prevent you retrieving it when you need to. Also, keep it clear of sharp edges that could cut into the rope.

If it is necessary to do a long abseil you may need to join two ropes, in which case try a double fisherman's knot. Avoid loose rock or sharp edges in the area where the rope will run, as the rope may become severed. Make sure that long hair and loose clothing do not get caught up in the abseiling devices and ropes.

Tie yourself and the top of the abseil rope to the anchor(s). If necessary – and to avoid abseiling off the end of the rope – tie a knot in the bottom end of the abseil rope before throwing the rope down the cliff. Make absolutely sure that anyone below is aware of what you are doing, and that the rope reaches down as far as the ledge you are trying to reach.

Pass the rope, from front to rear, between your legs, round your upper left thigh, diagonally across your chest, over your right shoulder, under your armpit and into your left hand. Walk slowly backwards over the edge, and crouch low if there is any danger of lifting the rope off the top of the anchor. The lower hand will control the braking – you should *never* try to brake with the upper hand. By turning your body outwards and towards your braking hand, you can make yourself more secure and also see downwards more clearly.

When descending, go down as smoothly as possible in order to avoid a pendulum effect that may draw the rope over a sharp edge. Once down, if pulling the rope through, beware of any rock that may be loosened by the rope.

Belaying

First of all, find an anchor. This could be a spike of rock, a tree or a jammed stone. Make a loop in the main rope and place it over or around the anchor point. The securing loop is formed using a figure-of-eight knot. You can also have a back-up anchor point for extra security.

Pass the rope over your head (so that it sits above the ropes linked to the anchors) and down to just above the hips, but below the softer part of the waist. Make a twist round the arm closest to the anchor, known as the dead arm. You should have covered arms as well as gloves, to reduce the danger of friction burns.

Take a seated position, with feet firmly anchored. Make sure the rope between you and the anchor is taut. You and the anchor should be in line with the direction of force. To stop a fall, bring the dead hand across the front of the body. Never take the dead hand off the rope when the rope is being paid out or drawn in. The live hand, nearest the climber, should do this work.

KNOTS

Greater detail on knots is given in Chapter 13, Ropes and Knots, but below are a few useful ones for climbing.

Overhand knot
Probably the simplest of all knots.

Double overhand knot
This is the same as the overhand knot but the end is taken twice round the ropes before being fed through.

Figure-of-eight
A versatile climbing knot which is easy to tie and untie. The knot should not be tied with too short a tail, and if the tail is short, tie a stopper knot on the end of it.

Bowline
This is a good way of tying on to the rope. Take care to tie it properly. Secure it with a stopper bound round the rope in the loop.

Fisherman's knot
The simplest way of joining two ropes consists of two overhand knots, tied round the other rope and pulled tight.

Double fisherman's knot
A more secure method of joining two ropes involves tying two double overhand knots round each rope and pulling tight.

Snow cave

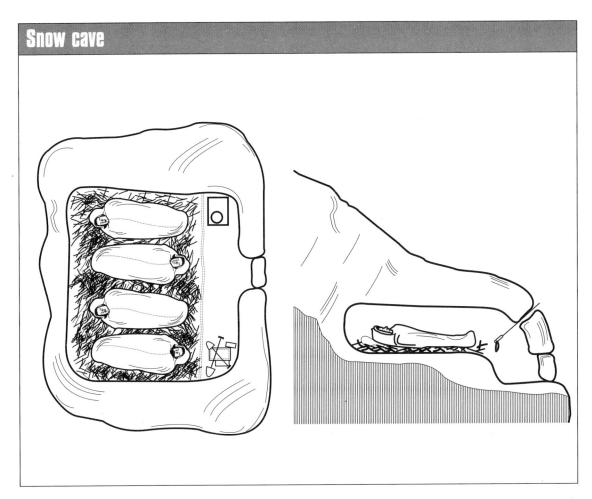

SHELTERING ON A MOUNTAIN

It is almost always wiser to use your time and energy to descend from a mountain than to dig a snow hole. However, one of your party may be injured, or there may be other pressing reasons why you cannot do this. If so, then the most sensible action is to look for a suitable snowdrift in the lee of a boulder or other natural feature and make yourself a snow cave.

Snow cave

Cut directly into the drift and then excavate cavities at either side to create the main chamber. Cutting the cavity out in blocks may be quicker than scraping out snow with a small axe. Use a rucksack to seal the entrance, which should be slightly lower than the main chamber. Remember to have a ventilation hole in the chamber, as well as ventilation through the entrance

CHAPTER SEVEN

Surviving Natural Disasters

Awareness is one of the keys for coping with natural disasters. You should be aware both of the potential dangers of the region you are in and of the correct course of action to take.

The better prepared you are, the easier it will be to cope with whatever nature can throw at you, and the more likely it is you will survive. If you are well prepared you are also in a better position to help others. It is difficult to think quickly and plan when an emergency is under way and people are panicking. If you have planned ahead and know where your essential equipment is, everything is much more likely to fall into place at the crucial moment.

Keep in touch with meteorological warnings. This may involve carrying a battery-powered radio. Make sure that you have emergency supplies to hand. These may include:

- Food and water.
- First aid kit.
- Pocket knife, eating utensils, can opener, etc.
- Map.
- Torch.
- Adequate clothing.
- Good shoes or boots.

EARTHQUAKE

Earthquakes are impossible to predict and can have a number of different classifications

– tectonic, volcanic and artificially produced. No place on earth is free from the danger of an earthquake.

Most earthquakes occur at the edges of tectonic plates. Plates either slide against each other, or one under the other, but there are plenty of examples of earthquakes that do not occur at the edges of plates.

Cities in danger of earthquake

Alexandria	Lisbon
Algiers	Los Angeles
Ankara	Managua
Athens	Manila
Bangkok	Mexico
Beijing (Peking)	Milan
Bogota	Nanking
Bucharest	Naples
Cairo	Osaka
Calcutta	Pyongyang
Canton	Rangoon
Caracas	Rome
Casablanca	San Francisco
Chongqing	Santiago
Davao	Seoul
Dacca	Shanghai
Guatemala City	Shenyang
Harbin	Sian
Havana	Singapore
Hong Kong	Surabaya
Istanbul	Taipei
Jakarta	Tashkent
Kabul	Teheran
Kanpur	Tientsin
Kobe	Tokyo
Kuala Lumpur	Tripoli
Kunming	Turin
Lahore	Wuhan
Lanzhou	Yokohama
Lima	

Recording an earthquake

THE RICHTER SCALE

FORCE OF EARTHQUAKE	SCALE
Not felt but recorded on seismometer	2.6
Widely felt	3.5
Local damage	4.5
Destructive earthquake	6.0
Major earthquake	7.0
Great earthquake	8.0+

THE MERCALLI SCALE

I.	Felt by almost no one.
II.	Felt by very few people.
III.	Tremor noticed, but not recognised as an earthquake.
IV.	Felt indoors by many.
V.	Felt by almost everyone. Trees and poles swaying.
VI.	Felt by everyone. Furniture moved. Slight damage.
VII.	Everyone runs out doors. Considerable damage to poorly built structures.
VIII.	Specially designed structures damaged. Others collapse.
IX.	All buildings considerably damaged. Cracks in ground.
X.	Many structures destroyed. Ground badly cracked.
XI.	Almost all structures fall. Bridges wrecked. Wide cracks in the ground.
XII.	Total destruction. Waves seen on ground.

Dangers

The danger of an earthquake is usually its effect on man-made structures or the triggering of such things as landslides and tidal waves (tsunamis).

Ground

Earthquake effects can be worse on soft

Earthquake and shockwave

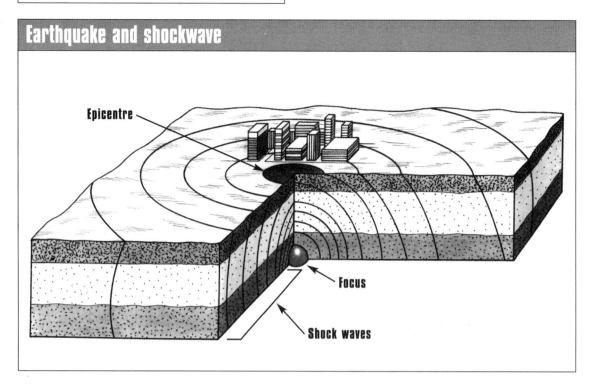

Epicentre

Focus

Shock waves

ground, which tends to amplify the shock-waves, particularly mud and clay soils. This also applies to water-logged, low-lying regions. Steep slopes can be perilous because of the danger of landslides.

Preparation
Put together essential supplies such as water, canned food, a battery-powered radio and a torch.

Action
Indoors
- If you are inside a building, get under a strong table or some other protection and hold on during the tremors.
- If you cannot get underneath something, get close to an inside wall.
- Keep away from heavy objects like book cases.
- Do not attempt to run out of a building during an earthquake, as you will be at great risk from falling and flying objects.

Saffir-Simpson scale of storm intensity

STORM CATEGORY	WIND SPEED (MPH)
Tropical storm	31–73
Hurricane Level 1	
(Weak)	74–95
Level 2	
(Moderate)	96–110
Level 3	
(Strong)	111–130
Level 4	
(Very strong)	131–155
Level 5	
(Devastating)	156–

- Keep away from any glass, such as windows or mirrors, that might shatter.

Outdoors

- Do not try to run away from the earthquake, as you are likely to run into danger.
- Keep away from trees, buildings or other structures that might fall on you.
- Keep clear of telephone poles, electricity pylons and wires. Never try to touch or move an electric cable that has fallen.

In a car

- Slow down and drive to a clear place, away from underpasses, lamp-posts or trees.
- Stay in the car until the shaking stops.

HURRICANE

A hurricane is a storm with winds of between 74 and 200mph (120 and 320km/h).

Hurricanes have their source in equatorial waters, particularly the Caribbean Sea and the Gulf of Mexico. In the western Pacific Ocean they are known as typhoons and in the Indian Ocean and around Australia they are known as tropical cyclones.

Dangers

The destructive power of a hurricane can be manifested in different ways, including wind power, tornadoes, rainfall and storm surges.

Formation of a hurricane

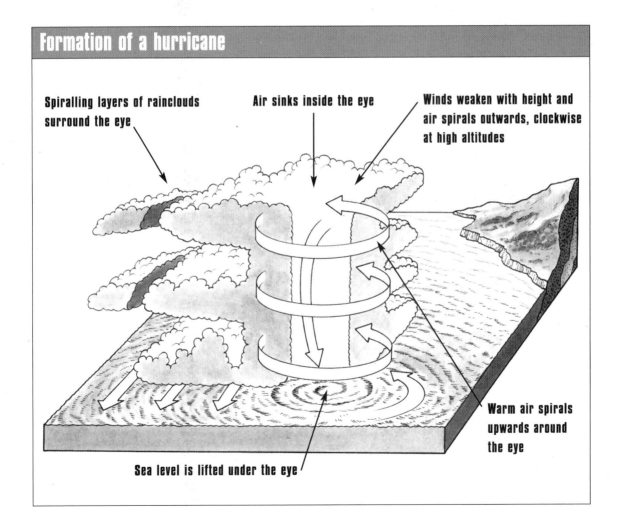

Spiralling layers of rainclouds surround the eye

Air sinks inside the eye

Winds weaken with height and air spirals outwards, clockwise at high altitudes

Warm air spirals upwards around the eye

Sea level is lifted under the eye

Fujita-Pearson tornado scale

F–0: 40–72mph (64–115km/h)	Chimney damage, tree branches broken
F–1: 73–112mph (116–179km/h)	Mobile homes overturned
F–2: 113–157mph (180–251km/h)	Considerable damage, mobile homes demolished, trees uprooted
F–3: 158–205mph (252–328km/h)	Roofs and walls torn down, trains overturned, cars thrown
F–4: 206–260mph (329–416km/h)	Well-constructed walls levelled
F–5: 261–318mph (417–509km/h)	Houses lifted off foundations and carried considerable distances; cars thrown as far as 330ft (100m)

The storm surge is the most dangerous aspect of the hurricane, accounting for 90 per cent of deaths. It is caused by changes in atmospheric pressure inside the hurricane sucking up the sea. Hurricane winds also pile up the water against the coastlines. The resulting wall of water can be up to 40ft (12m) high, though it diminishes as it heads inland.

Forecast

It is difficult to forecast a hurricane. Even meteorological offices in developed countries can be caught with their guard down, with devastating consequences..

Hurricanes tend to be more prolific in the Atlantic region in August and September. The source of the hurricane consists of warm water influenced by the earth's rotation. The sea temperature must be at least 79°F (26°C). Hurricanes occur at least 4–5° pole-wards from the equator, and no closer.

When there is a threat of a hurricane occuring within the next 24–36 hours, a Hurricane Watch is issued. If a hurricane is expected in less than 24 hours a Hurricane Warning is issued. During a hurricane watch, listen to a battery-powered radio for updates and make preparations.

Preparation

- Board up windows in a building.
- Taping up windows will not help.
- Trim any weak branches off trees that may be near houses.

- Bring inside any objects, such as garbage cans or garden chairs, that the wind could pick up.

Action
Inside

- Shelter in the cellar or somewhere away from windows or the roof. A hurricane can rip off the roof.
- Do not drop your guard when the calm eye of the storm passes over. The other side of the storm, with winds travelling in the opposite direction, will soon reach you.

Outside

- Find a cave, ditch or rocky outcrop to shelter in or under.
- Be prepared to adjust your position when the eye of the storm has passed over.
- Do not attempt to drive anywhere in a car in a hurricane.
- Take care with bridges, which may be washed away.

TORNADO

Hurricanes can spawn tornadoes, which are much more unpredictable. The track of a tornado is erratic, and so all the more dangerous. A tornado will not give you time to plan and think. Be ready to act fast.

A tornado looks like a grey spiral, funnel or elephant's trunk, and wind speeds can be anything from 300 to 350mph (480 to

560km/h). It is made visible by the dust that is sucked up by the winds and by condensed water droplets. The area of the tornado touching the ground is usually only a few hundred feet/metres across, though it can be up to half a mile (1km) wide. A tornado can cause a house to tear apart by creating higher pressure inside the house than outside.

Preparation

Find a cellar or tornado shelter in good time before the storm arrives. Remember that, even if the tornado does not appear to be heading in your direction, it may suddenly change course.

Action
Inside

- Shelter in the basement or lowest level of the building.
- Stay in the centre of the room, away from corners and windows.
- Shelter under strong furniture, such as a heavy table, and hold on.
- Protect your head and neck with your arms.
- If you are in a mobile home or trailer.

Outside

- Do not walk around outside as you could be plucked up by the wind or be struck by heavy objects thrown by the wind.
- Do not stay in a car, but get out and find the most solid shelter available.
- Shelter in a ditch if necessary or under a sturdy rocky outcrop.

LIGHTNING

Lightning is a visible electrical discharge between clouds, or between a cloud and the earth. More people in the developed world are killed by lightning than by any other natural phenomenon. It is, however, easier to protect yourself from lightning than from an earthquake or a hurricane.

Prediction

Although there is such a thing as a bolt from the blue (lightning out of a clear, blue sky), the most likely source of lightning is dark thunderclouds. If you see them approaching, take precautions.

Lightning is accompanied by thunder. Since light travels faster than sound, you can estimate the distance in miles between yourself and a thunderstorm by counting the seconds that elapse between the lightning and the thunder, and dividing by five. You are still in danger from lightning, even if the storm is far away.

Protection

You can protect a building from lightning by attaching a metallic rod, wired to the ground, to the highest part of the roof.

Action
Inside

- Stay away from telephones, electrical appliances, computers and, in particular, televisions.
- Do not use faucets in sinks or bathtubs because metal pipes and water conduct electricity.

Outside

- Do not shelter under a single tree, as the lightning is likely to strike the tree.
- Lie flat on the ground if you are exposed in a thunderstorm.
- Find a ditch or depression to lie in.
- If you feel your hair standing on end out in the open, bend forward and put your hands on your knees. Adopt a low crouching position with your feet together and hands on ears to minimise thunder shock. Remove any metal objects.
- If you need to take shelter in a cave, make sure you go deep inside if possible. Do not stay near the mouth of the cave.
- Avoid water.
- Avoid high ground.
- Avoid open spaces.

FLOOD

Floods are a common and very dangerous form of natural disaster, especially for the large part of the earth's population that live beside coasts, river deltas and estuaries.

After rainfall, water is absorbed by the soil and vegetation, or by evaporation. The remainder, called the runoff, runs into streams and rivers. When the runoff is too large, and streams and rivers cannot contain it, a flood is caused. Intense rainfall over a small area causes flash floods.

Preparation

Find out about water level at flood stage in the place you are staying. Fill bathtubs, sinks and buckets with clean water, in case the water supply becomes contaminated. Keep in touch with flood warnings on a battery-operated radio.

Action
Inside

- Collect vital supplies and move to an upper part of the house. Be prepared, if necessary, to climb out on to the roof. Take warm clothing.
- Take some rope with you to tie yourself and others to a stable structure like a chimney stack if you are on the roof.

Outside

- Make your way to high ground.
- Do not, if at all possible, wade through flood water. If absolutely necessary, perform the routine for river crossings as described in Chapter 12, Rafts and River Crossings.
- If you are in a vehicle that has stalled, abandon it and get to high ground as quickly as possible.

TSUNAMI

Tidal waves called tsunamis are caused by earthquakes with vertical movement that create water displacement.

Prediction

It is difficult to predict a tsunami from the behaviour of waves at sea, since tsunami waves might travel a long way at a height of no more than 3ft (1m) and therefore pass by ships unnoticed. When they reach land, however, they can be about 50ft (15m) high. Japan's worst tsunami involved a wave 80ft (24m) high.

Tsunami alerts are issued on the basis of earthquake reports. Although this system can work well for places that are far enough away from the earthquake, it is often the case that the tsunami will have struck before the warning can be given.

Keep in touch with earthquake warnings, and beware any unusual rumblings.

Preparation

Plan an escape route to an inland location that is above the likely height of any approaching wave. Put together an emergency kit with food and first aid.

Action

- Do not head towards the beach to check if you can see a wave approaching. If you can see it, it is too late to escape.
- Remember that a series of waves may be involved, so do not return to the danger area until there is a complete all-clear.

DROUGHT

The average person needs 2US/1¾UK pints (1litre) of water per day to stay alive. The human diet requires about 300 tons (304 metric tonnes) of water to grow the necessary food for each person's annual intake.

In the United States drought is defined as less than 0.09ins (2.5mm) of rainfall in 48 hours. In Britain an absolute drought is defined as a period of 15 days with less than 0.009ins (0.25mm) of rain each day. In India a drought is declared if the rainfall is less than 75 per cent of the average.

Major droughts tend to occur at latitudes of about 15–20°, in areas which border on

Types of drought

METEOROLOGICAL DROUGHT	Unusual precipitation for a certain region during a certain time scale.
AGRICULTURAL DROUGHT	Inadequate soil moisture for the growth of particular plants in certain regions.
HYDROLOGICAL DROUGHT	Reduced precipitation for an extended period; usual water supplies, such as lakes, rivers and reservoirs, are deficient.
SOCIOECONOMIC DROUGHT	Water supplies are so low that the community is adversely affected.

the permanently dry areas of the world. Due to unpredictable rainfall, Africa is more at the mercy of droughts than any other area. Seasonal rainfall in Africa can show large variations within the season, and tends to fall in short and intense storms. The rain can also be very localised.

Preparation

You will need to have a store of water and take care that water supplies do not become contaminated during a drought. Ensure that all water is boiled before drinking.

(See Chapter 2, Survival in the Desert, for more tips on finding water in arid regions.)

FIRE

Aridity and drought can lead to bush fires. Australia is especially prone to these, with the native eucalyptus tree being a prime culprit in the spread of fire. There tends to be a great deal of dry bark and other matter on the floor of Australian forests, providing good fuel for fires. The amount of litter and the time that has elapsed since the last fire are critical in judging how intensely a fire will burn.

Prevention

- Take great care when lighting a camp fire, especially in a dry area.
- Use a constructed fireplace or light the fire in a trench at least 1ft (30cm) deep.
- Take care that tree roots do not catch fire.

Types of fire

GROUND FIRE	Burns below the surface of the earth in layers of organic material such as peat. They tend to smoulder, have no flame and little smoke. They are difficult to control.
SURFACE FIRE	Includes grass fires and forest fires that burn debris on the forest floor. They can also burn the lower branches of trees.
CROWN FIRE	Burns the tops of trees, and they are dangerously unpredictable. They can burn ahead of the surface fire.
SPOT FIRE	Caused by burning leaves and bark being blown ahead of the main fire, and causing secondary fires elsewhere, sometimes many kilometres away.

- Clear the ground in the area at least 10ft (3m) from the camp fire.
- Do not light a fire when conditions are hot and windy, and when the bush is very dry.

If you see a fire starting, use a branch with

Recommended safety area around a camp fire in a forest

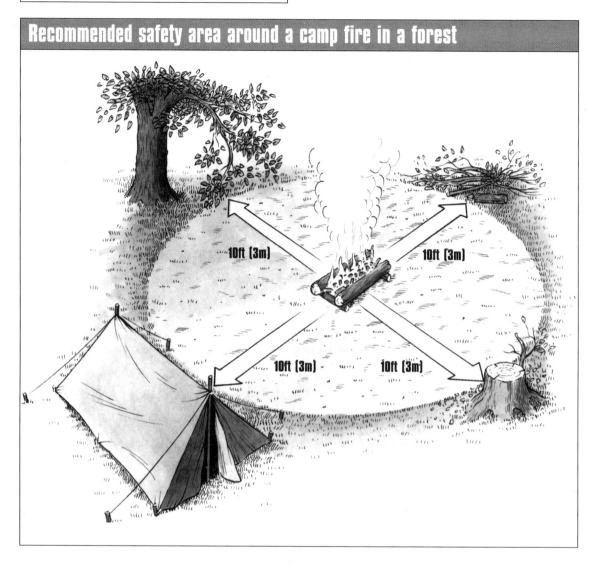

10ft (3m)   10ft (3m)

10ft (3m)   10ft (3m)

green leaves to damp it down or use any available fire-fighting equipment, such as poles with flaps on the end that can be found in most forests. Do not swing the flames around and thus spread the fire. Remember that fires burn more rapidly uphill and that burnt material can roll down the hill.

Action

If you are trapped by a fire:

- Try to crouch in a pond, lake or river.
- Look for shelter in a clear area or among rocks.
- Lie flat and cover your body and head with wet clothing or with soil.
- Breathe the air close to the ground to avoid scorching your lungs or inhaling smoke.
- As a last resort, if you see an opening, and the fire is not too deep or too high, you can attempt to dash through the flames to the area behind them that has already been burnt. You will need to be absolutely

resolved to go all the way through and not try to turn back, so be sure. If the flames are higher than head height, do not attempt to run through them.

- If you decide to dash through the flames, cover as much of the surface of your body as possible and dampen clothes and hair if you have water.
- If your clothes catch light, do not stay on your feet once out of the fire, but crouch down.
- Do not try to escape a fire by running uphill, unless absolutely necessary.

VOLCANO

Volcanoes are formed by the outpouring of lava and by other fragment material. There are a number of active volcanoes around the world and some volcanoes, such as Vesuvius, are dormant.

Dangers

When a volcano erupts, lava mixed with steam and other gases is forced out of the earth and forms an impenetrable cloud. The lava rises inside the vent of the volcano, some pieces shoot up into the air and other lava flows over the crater. Some lava may emerge from a secondary vent in the side of the volcano.

The lava flow is generally slow-moving, though this is not always the case. *Pahoehoe* is a smooth lava that forms a ropy surface. *Aa* is sharp and twisted, much like clinker, and tends to flow faster than pahoehoe. The latter flows at about 3ft (1m) per minute, though if the slope is steep and the lava emission is heavy, this speed can increase to 400 metres per minute, or 14mph, which can overtake a person.

Aa tends to move in surges, piling up each time before moving on. As well as lava, the volcano can throw out material which ranges from fine ash to 8-tonne bombs that can travel up to three miles. This flying material, or pyroclastic flow, is the most dangerous

element of the the volcano, since the lava itself, with a certain amount of warning, can be avoided without too much difficulty.

Another highly destructive characteristic of some volcanoes is *nuees ardentes*, or glowing clouds. These are ground-hugging clouds of molten lava fragments that can move with great speed down a mountain.

Secondary effects

Secondary effects from a volcano include earthquakes (normally preceding the eruption), flash floods, landslides and mudflows, thunderstorms and tsunamis.

In Colombia, in 1985, a volcano precipitated a landslide of mud and rock which buried a whole town and its inhabitants. Since the soil on the edges of volcanoes is fertile, larger numbers of people than ever before are willing to take the risk of living in the danger area. The presence of other people does not mean it is safe.

Prediction

It is difficult to predict accurately a volcanic eruption, just as it is difficult to predict an earthquake. One of the best indications of timing is the record of the particular volcano, which will give a fair idea of when it is likely to erupt again. An earthquake almost invariably precedes an eruption, though the timescale can vary from hours to months.

Preparation

Be aware of the warning systems in your area. Remember that some countries have better warning systems than others, so be prepared to make your own judgements about danger signs when necessary. Always err on the side of caution, since even highly experienced volcanologists have been killed by volcanoes.

Make sure you have an evacuation plan prepared. Ideally, this should involve getting to high ground as far away from the eruption as possible. Also prepare an alternative route.

Volcanoes 1

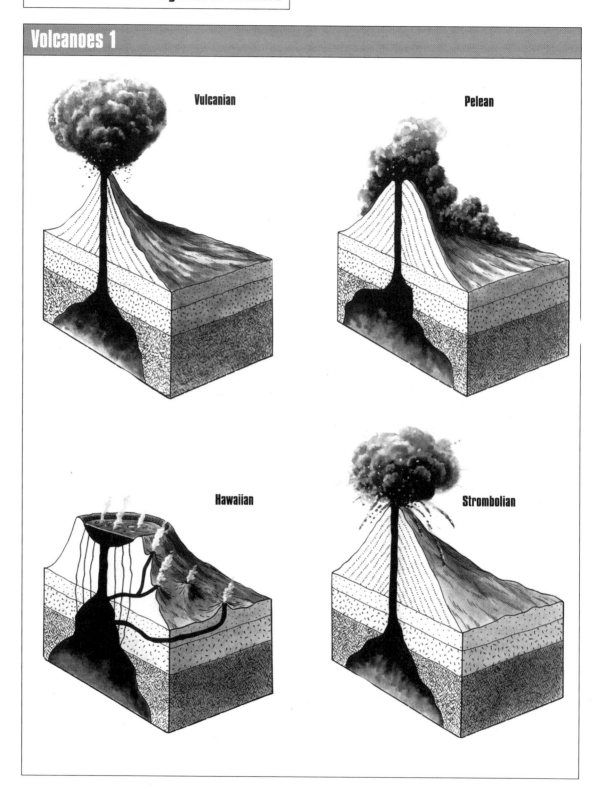

Vulcanian

Pelean

Hawaiian

Strombolian

Volcanoes 2

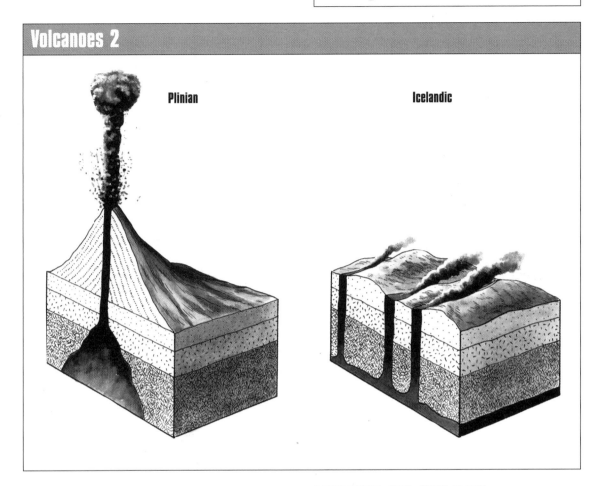

Plinian

Icelandic

Action

- Equip yourself with goggles and some kind of breathing mask. If you do not have a mask, hold a damp cloth over your face to help you breathe.
- Avoid low-lying areas if possible, as you will be in danger from flash floods.
- Do not cross a low-lying area or go over a bridge if there is a mud-flow approaching. You cannot outrun a mud-flow.

Aftermath

- Beware of inhaling ash – keep a mask on or use a damp cloth.
- Keep goggles on.
- Beware of the danger of heavy ash, which can collapse roofs, etc.

LANDSLIDE AND MUD-FLOW

Prediction

There is usually little or no warning of a landslide or mud-flow, but the following signs can be an indication.

Inside

- Doors stick; cracks appear in plaster, tiles, bricks, etc.

Outside

- Cracks begin to appear in the ground and pavement; water comes out of the ground in places that it normally doesn't; fences and trees move; there is a rumbling sound.

Action

Inside

- Shelter under a sturdy object, such as a table, and hold on.

Outside

- Get out of the path of the landslide or mud-flow (remember, you cannot outrun it).
- Head for the nearest high ground, which is out of the direct path of danger.
- If you are caught, curl up in a ball and protect your head.

BEWARE

There may be a mulitude of accidents waiting to happen after any of the above emergencies have occured. Watch out for the following:

- Fallen power lines, which could electrocute you if you touch them. There may be damage to electrical systems within buildings.
- Ruptured gas mains.
- Fires and floods.
- Dangerous flammable or toxic fluids and materials.
- Ruptured water pipes and contaminated water.
- Burst sewage pipes.
- Aftershocks that can bring down weakened structures.
- Animals, even tame ones, becoming more dangerous. Treat all animals with caution.

Use your common sense, and proceed with caution. Finally, do not forget to help others in need, such as children and the elderly.

VEHICLE PREPARATION AND MAINTENANCE

You will greatly reduce the danger of becoming stuck in a remote area if you have checked and maintained your vehicle properly. It is also wise to receive some training in off-road driving, or read a manual on the subject.

Checks

Things to check:

- Engine oil level.
- Radiator water level.
- Water in washer canisters.
- Battery water level and terminals.
- Power steering fluid level.
- Windshield-wiper blades and jets.
- Lights.
- Tyre pressures and condition of tyres and wheels.

For long journeys and expeditions you will need to be confident that the following items are in working order:

Electrical

Lights, fuse boxes, spark plugs, distributor cap and rotor arm, condenser, starter motor and alternator.

Body and fittings

Springs, shock absorbers, chassis and engine/gearbox mounts, half-shafts, differentials, brake drums, brake calipers, brake pads/shoes, clutch, radiator, water hoses, thermostat, water pump.

Also make sure that you are able to carry out at least routine servicing or replacements in the field. This may mean attending a vehicle-maintenance course.

Oil, lubricants and filters

Filters for oil, fuel and air, brake and clutch fluids, oil for engine, gearbox, transfer box, differentials and hubs.

Additional equipment

New and spare tyres (adapted to the environment), lights, batteries, lockable boxes and padlocks, additional fuel tank, roof rack with jerry can holders if necessary, and engine snorkel.

Tools

Wrenches/spanners, hammer, feeler gauge,

Landslides and mud-flows

Mud-flow

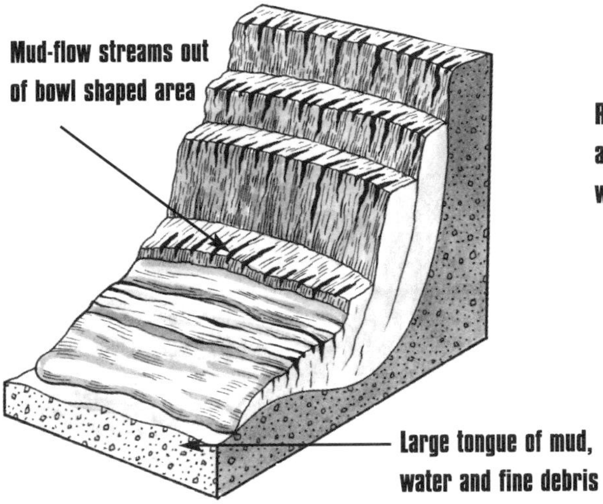

Mud-flow streams out of bowl shaped area

Large tongue of mud, water and fine debris

Rockfall

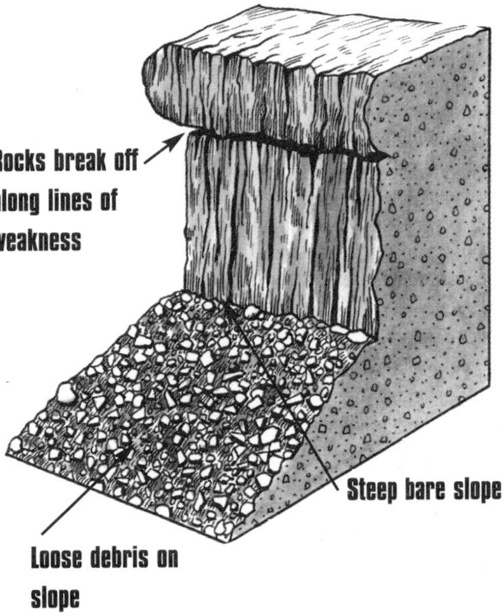

Rocks break off along lines of weakness

Steep bare slope

Loose debris on slope

Slump

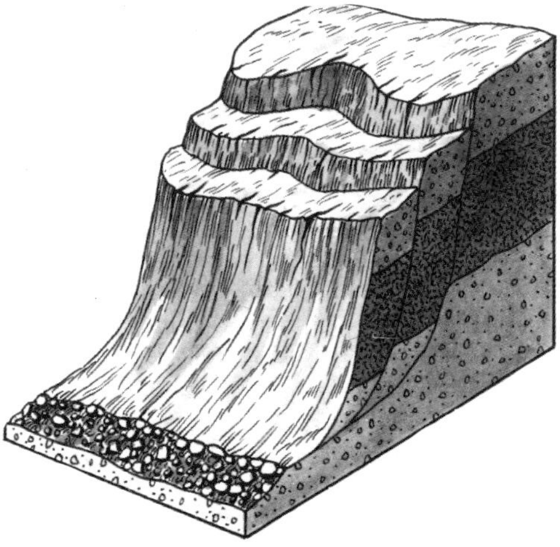

Landslide

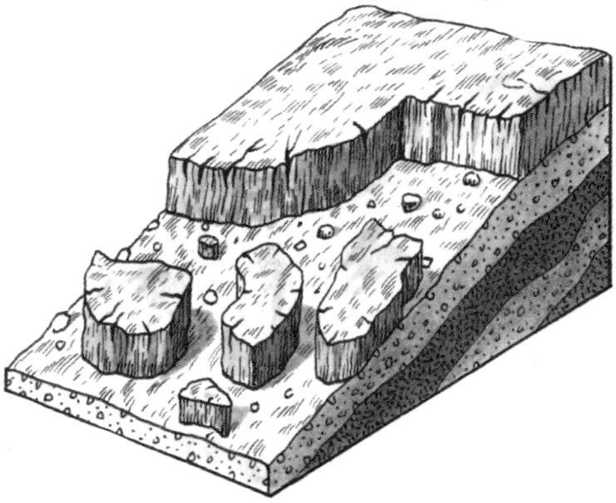

grease gun, pump, spare nuts and bolts, hose clips, tape, torque wrench, puncture repair kit, jump leads, tool roll, ratchet set with spark plugs, axle stands with off-road pads, tyre levers, valve tool and spare valves and exhaust repair gum.

Spares

You will need to gauge the likely availability of spares for the particular make of vehicle in the region you will be driving in. Check the dealer network. Typical spares may include:

Brake and indicator lights, inner tubes, alternator, headlamp, radiator sealant and flush, shock absorbers, power-steering fluid, engine oil, fan belts, thermostat, wheel bearings, gaskets, wing mirror, brake shoes/pads, water hoses.

Vehicle recovery

The following items may be required if you get your vehicle stuck in mud, ice or sand:

Winch, large bow and D-shackles, tow-rope, kinetic recovery rope, high-lift jack with jacking plate, spade.

Vehicle protection

Depending on the kind of terrain you will be negotiating, you may need some or all of the following:

Bull bars, sump guard, sand channels, armoured brake hoses, light covers, roll cage.

DRIVING OFF-ROAD

In general you will want to keep the vehicle moving and have maximum traction. Do not drive too fast off-road and try not to come to a halt in a soft area, such as mud or sand, which will cause wheel spin.

Getting stuck

If you do come to a halt and the wheels start spinning, take your foot off the accelerator immediately and plan what to do next. If you keep the wheels spinning the vehicle will simply dig deeper into the hole. If stuck in a soft area, first of all try reversing out slowly. If the vehicle still does not move, try rocking it gently in a forward gear to try to tease it out of the hole.

If this does not work, get out of the vehicle and consider whether it will be possible to place brushwood or stones under the wheels to improve traction. You may have the option of either towing the vehicle out with another vehicle, or using a winch with one end attached to the front of your vehicle and the other to a solid object, such as a tree.

When towing or winching, make sure any bystanders are well out of reach of the length of the towing cable in case it should snap.

Winching

- Keep bystanders well clear.
- If you are in the vehicle, raise the bonnet for protection.
- Wear strong gloves when handling the cable.
- Wear boots with good grip so that you do not slip over.
- Put a piece of canvas on the middle of the cable to reduce recoil if the cable breaks.
- Place the winch sling low round a tree or rock.

Ruts

Drive across ruts at a diagonal in order to keep all four wheels on the ground and provide the maximum traction. If the ruts are not too deep, you can drive along them rather like a train. Take care of sudden spins on the wheel and try not to fight the direction of the ruts. If they are too deep, you will need to place one side of the wheels on the top of one of the ruts and the other side of the wheels on the verge. Take care not to slip off these two supports.

Sand

Sand becomes progressively more difficult to drive on as it becomes drier during the day.

The tyres can be deflated to a pressure of about 12 pounds (5kg) per square inch to aid sand travel but remember that this also reduces ground clearance.

If the vehicle enters soft sand, change to four-wheel drive and keep the vehicle moving evenly, changing down smoothly when necessary, and keeping the wheels as straight as possible.

Water

To drive through water you will need to check the vehicle is waterproofed in the vital areas, such as the electrics and any breathing tubes. Wade across the water obstacle with ropes attached and carefully check the depth of the water, the strength of the current and for any hidden obstacles. You will need to ensure that any loose items either in or on the vehicle are securely lashed down.

The crossing should be performed at a low and constant speed until the vehicle is well clear of the water. Check over the vehicle and remember that there will be a temporary reduction in braking efficiency for a while after leaving the water.

Hills

A four-wheel-drive vehicle is normally high-sided and therefore relatively easy to tip over. Hills should therefore be negotiated straight up or down in the appropriate gear for the steepness of slope. Make sure you stay in the same gear and keep the momentum up when ascending. If you have to retreat, hold the vehicle on the brake and select reverse gear. Come down the slope backwards in reverse gear under engine control. When descending, keep the vehicle under engine braking power and do not suddenly apply the brakes, which could cause the vehicle to skid.

CHAPTER EIGHT

First Aid

You can go a long way towards saving somebody's life with only a basic knowledge of First Aid. This can be picked up from books, though finding a centre that can provide practical training is probably the best option.

The sequence for administering First Aid should be as follows:
1. Is it safe?
2. Rapid assessment: ABC (Airway, Breathing, Circulation).
3. If necessary, institute immediate resuscitation.
4. Recovery position, if appropriate.
5. Full assessment: examination techniques.
6. Stabilize condition and get help as needed.

IS IT SAFE?

The first thing to ask yourself when you come across a victim is: 'Is it safe?' This means that you should consider whether you will be risking your own life in rushing to the aid of the victim, for example by running into a busy road.

Once you have checked the potential risks, move the victim to a safe place, e.g. dragging them off a road or away from a rock-fall. You may need to remove a dangerous object from the vicinity of the victim, making sure you do not put your own life at risk in the process.

RAPID ASSESSMENT: ABC

ABC stands for Airway, Breathing, Circulation. These three must be checked – and in that order – properly to assess the victim's condition.

Airway

Check that the airways are open and clear, and that there are no obstructions, such as blood, vomit, loose teeth, etc. Check that the tongue has not fallen back down the throat. Use a gudel airway if necessary.

Breathing

Look to see that the chest is rising and falling. Listen for the sound of breathing. Feel with hand in front of nose and mouth for exhaled air.

Mouth-to-mouth resuscitation

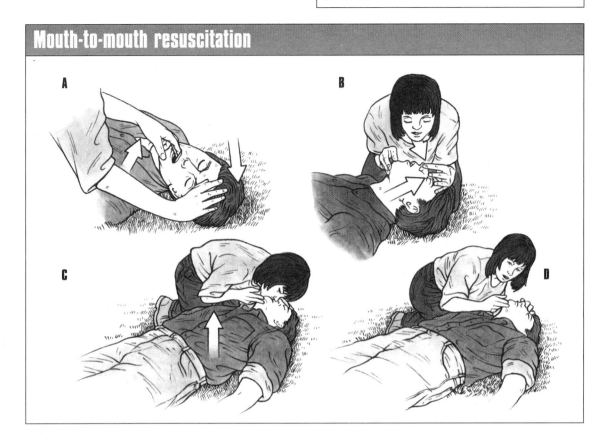

Circulation

Check for a pulse. Is the pulse strong and regular? Check for major blood loss. Institute immediate resuscitation, if necessary.

ARTIFICIAL RESPIRATION

If the victim is not breathing, he or she will die in a short time. You must, therefore, restore breathing immediately.

After clearing the airway of any blockages and ensuring the victim is on a reasonably firm surface (A), tilt the victim's head backwards and place the heel of your hand on the forehead of the victim so that the chin is raised. With the hand resting on the forehead, pinch the victim's nose with thumb and forefinger (B). Take a deep breath, place your mouth tightly over the victim's mouth and blow air from yours into their mouth (C). Stop blowing when the victim's chest is expanded (D).

Lift your hand from the victim and watch for the chest to fall. Give the victim further quick breaths, taking a deep breath yourself between each one. Carry on blowing into the victim's lungs at a rate of 12 breaths per minute until the victim begins to breathe on

Skin discolouration

COLOURING	LIKELY CAUSE
Ruddy	Poisoning
Yellow	Jaundiced
Blue	Cyanosis (lack of oxygen)
Greenish	Nauseous
Black	Bruising
White	Blocked vessel to peripheral organ

Cardio-pulmonary massage

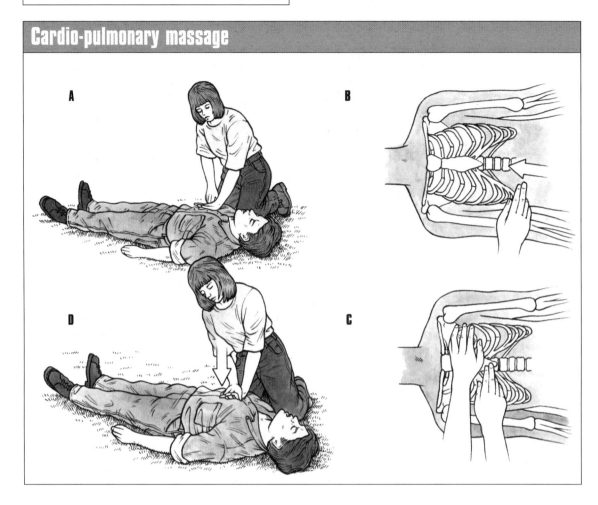

his or her own. You can then stop blowing at this stage.

EXAMINATION TECHNIQUES

The basic sequence when assessing a victim, unless the symptoms are obvious, is – LOOK, FEEL, LISTEN.

If you are examining a limb joint, the sequence is: LOOK, FEEL, MOVE.

A general examination should take into account the victim's weight and general fitness, their skin tone and their psychological state.

Lie the patient down and examine the following, from the right of the body. Reassure the patient continuously.

Hands check nails and palms for anaemia.

Pulse check the rate, rhythm and volume.

Blood pressure hypotension is low, hypertension is high.

Head eyes, ears, lips and mouth.

Neck check not broken or bruised.

Chest lungs and heart.

Abdomen liver, spleen, kidneys.

Limbs look, feel, move.

CARDIO-PULMONARY RESUSCITATION

This method is used when the patient has stopped breathing and when there is no pulse. It should only be performed by someone who has had training in the method. Never perform this technique if there is even a trace of a pulse.

If after performing artificial resuscitation the victim's heart is still not beating, place the heel of one hand on the lower part of the breastbone and place the other hand on top (A). Take care when you apply pressure not to damage the ribs (B). You should compress the breastbone 80 times per minute, with a pause every 15 to give the victim two breaths (C and D).

If there are two people available to help, one should perform the chest compression and the other mouth-to-mouth respiration. This should be at a ratio of one breath per five compressions. You should give 60 compressions per minute with a pause of one to one and a half seconds after every five compressions.

Children and infants

You should exert less pressure and increase the number of compressions per minute. Use two fingers on an infant, compressing 100 times per minute. Take care only to depress to about 1in (2.5cm). With children up to 10 years, use the heel of one hand and push lightly 90–100 times per minute. Only compress by 1½ins (3.5cm). You should give 5 compressions for every lung inflation.

CHOKING

Choking is caused by a blockage of the airway, often by food. Signs of choking are a person holding their throat, an inability to cough, a wheezing sound, blue skin (if unconscious), no rise and fall of the chest (if unconscious).

Conscious victim

Lower the victim's head to below chest level and then administer some blows to the back (A). They should be firm but take care not to damage the spine. If this does not work, stand behind the victim and place one fist just under the breastbone or sternum (B). Hold the fist with the other hand, and then make a sharp, hard thrusting movement inwards and upwards (C). If you are alone and you are choking, administer abdominal thrusts to yourself with your hands (D) or use a blunt projection, for example, a tree stump or, if you are indoors, the back of a chair.

Unconscious victim

Place the heel of one of your hands against the middle of his or her abdomen, just above the navel. Place the other hand on top, and press with a quick upward thrust. If the obstacle is not freed, try removing it with a finger or an instrument such as a pair of forcepts or tweezers. Use a torch if necessary to examine the upper airway. If the victim stays unconscious, call for help. If there is no breathing, use artificial respiration.

Infant

Straddle the baby over your arm with the head below the level of the rest of the body. Support the baby's head by holding its jaw. Give the baby four firm blows between the shoulder blades, taking care not to damage its spine or bruise it.

RECOVERY POSITION

If there is any danger of spinal injury, particularly to the neck, the spine should be immobilised before moving. If there is no danger of spinal injury, place the victim in the recovery postion, which will stop them choking.

Turn the head of the victim towards you, tilting it back slightly so as to open the airway. Put the arm that is nearer to you by the side of the victim and slide it under their buttock. Lay the other arm across the victim's chest.

Then place the leg that is further away from you across the one that is nearer to you

Choking

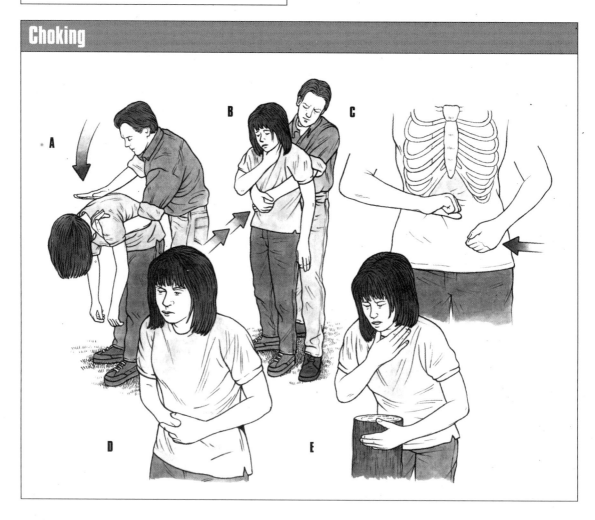

at the ankle. Pull the victim gently towards you by grasping clothing around the hip with one hand, and support the head with the other hand. Rest the victim against your knees. Bend the top-side leg so that the body does not roll. Keep the head tilted back to maintain an open airway.

NEAR DROWNING
Signs of near drowning include:
- Pale and cool skin.
- No breathing.
- Blue lips (cyanosis).
- Weak or absent pulse.
- Unconsciousness.

Treatment
ABC – Airway, Breathing, Circulation.
CPR – Cardio-Pulmonary Resuscitation if the victim has no pulse.
Treatment for hypothermia.
Treatment for shock.

It is vital that you keep the head lower than the rest of the body in order to allow water to drain naturally from the lungs.

If the patient is coughing and spluttering, turn him/her on their side. If he/she is unconscious, use the recovery position (see diagram opposite). Then call for medical assistance.

Recovery position

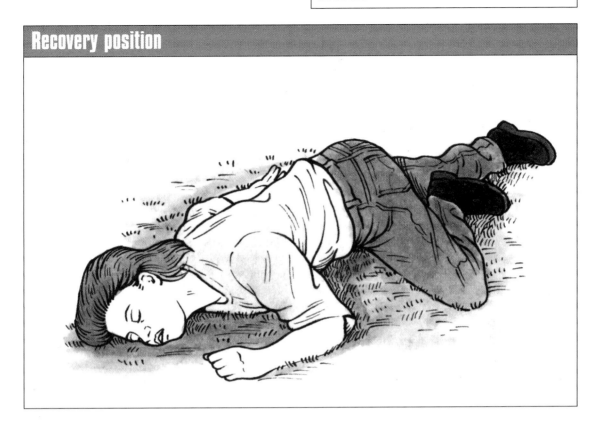

BLEEDING

Severe loss of blood will lead to shock (see below). Bleeding can be arterial, venous or capillary, in order of seriousness.

Arterial

Blood in the arteries is under high pressure, and therefore if an artery is ruptured the victim is in danger of a fatal loss of blood, and could die within minutes. Arterial blood can be recognised by its bright red colour and by the spurting effect in time with the pumping of the heart.

Venous

Venous blood is more easily controlled than arterial blood, and is a darker shade of red.

Capillary

The blood vessels opened in minor cuts and grazes.

Severe wounds

First of all apply direct pressure to the wound in order to stop the flow of blood. You will need to allow enough time for the wound to seal itself. Apply a sterile dressing with firm pressure to control the bleeding. If bleeding continues, do not remove the first dressing but add other dressings on top, as appropriate. If there is no fracture or dislocation, try to raise the limb that has been wounded and support it.

Another, less effective way of controlling bleeding is by using pressure points to seal off an artery above the wound. You should apply pressure at the end of the joint just above the injured area. On the hands, feet and head, this will be the wrist, ankle and neck respectively.

Cuts and Grazes

If there is a slight cut, try to rinse the wound

in clean water to remove any grit or dirt. Dab it gently with sterile gauze to dry it and apply a dressing or plaster.

Internal bleeding

Signs of internal bleeding may include frothy, bright-red blood coughed up by the victim (indicating bleeding in the lungs) or red blood in vomit (indicating bleeding in the stomach). Internal bleeding may be less obvious than external bleeding, in which case you can make deductions about what is likely to have resulted internally from the type of accident the victim suffered or the areas of bruising or tenderness.

Other signs and symptoms of internal bleeding include:
- Pale, clammy skin.
- Rapid and weak pulse.
- Rapid, shallow breathing.
- Tenderness in the abdomen.
- Any pain or discomfort.
- Nausea and/or vomiting.
- Shock.

If you suspect internal bleeding, lay the victim down with their legs elevated and their knees bent. Remember, all a person's blood can be lost in the body cavities. Call for medical assistance. Do not give anything by mouth.

WOUNDS

Open wounds need to be treated with great care in a survival situation because of the danger of contamination and the difficulties in keeping things clean. Remove any clothing from around the wound, if necessary by cutting it away. Clean the skin round the wound and irrigate the wound to remove any dirt. Cover it with a clean dressing, which should be changed daily to check for infection.

If the wound does become infected, place a warm moist compress on it and hold it there for 30 minutes. Allow the wound to drain. Then dress and bandage the wound again. If maggots get in the wound, you can leave them for as long as they are feeding on dead tissue. Pain and redness indicate that they have begun to feed on live tissue, in which case the maggots should be flushed out with sterile water or urine.

General rules for applying dressings
- The dressing pad should always extend well beyond the wound's edges.
- Place dressings directly on a wound. Do not slide them from the side, and replace any that slip out of place.
- If blood seeps through a dressing, do not remove it; instead, apply another dressing over the top.
- If there is only one sterile dressing, use this to cover the wound, and use other materials as top dressings.

Applying sterile dressings
- Remove the wrapping. Unwind the bandage's loose end, taking care not to drop the roll or touch the dressing pad.
- Unfold the dressing pad, holding the bandage on each side of the pad. Put the pad directly on the wound.
- Wind the short end of the bandage once around the limb and the dressing to secure the pad. Then, leave it hanging.
- Wind the other end of the bandage around the limb to cover the whole pad, leaving the tail hanging free.
- To secure the bandage, tie the ends in a reef knot, tied over the pad to exert firm pressure on the wound.
- Check the circulation to the extremity of the injured limb. Loosen bandage if necessary.

Adhesive dressing

If it is a gaping wound, you can use adhesive tape cut in the closure form of a butterfly clip to bring the sides of the wound together. Ensure the wound is thoroughly clean and sterile before closure. If necessary, and if you have confidence and training, you can use sutures.

Suturing a wound

Ensure there are no pockets of air or blood left below the skin. Make sure all materials used are clean. Pass the needle into one edge of the skin, through the full depth of the wound and out of the other edge. Knot each stitch at one side. Take in equal amounts of skin on both sides to align the edges of the wound.

Tie the sutures with a square knot. Loop over the needle holder, grasp the end through the loop and pull tight; loop round the needle holder in the opposite direction, grasp the end through the loop and pull tight again.

You should leave the sutures in place for about ten days. When you take them out, grasp the knot with forceps and tweezers and pull the stitch out with a firm pull.

BOILS

Apply warm compresses for long enough to allow the boil to develop into a head. You can then cut into the boil with a sterile knife or other sharp instrument (hold the blade over a flame first to sterilise it) to allow the pus to drain away. The pus should be thoroughly washed out with soap and water. Cover the wound and check it periodically while it heals.

RASHES

Rashes can be treated in different ways according to the cause. The general rule is: keep it dry if it is moist, and keep it moist if it is dry. A rash should be dressed and cared for in the same way as an open wound.

Severe burns

- Cool the area with water for 10 to 20 minutes or use a burn gel.
- Make the victim as comfortable as possible, protecting the wound from dirt.
- Do not remove anything that is sticking to the burn.
- Do not apply lotions, ointments, butter or fat to the injury.
- Provide adequate fluid for the victim to drink.
- Get help as soon as possible.

SHOCK

This is the rapid lowering of blood pressure owing to the lack of circulating volume to vital body organs, such as the brain, heart, liver and kidneys. If the victim has suffered burns they will have lost plasma. If they have suffered from vomiting or diarrhoea, they will have lost water. The effects

Burns

TYPE OF BURN	DAMAGE	TREATMENT
First-degree	Top layer of skin, e.g. sunburn. Skin turns red and then peels off.	Rehydrating creams. Treatment for restlessness, headache or fever – cool water at regular intervals.
Second-degree	Deeper damage to the skin, causing blisters. Shock.	Use antibacterial dressing, or leave wound undressed but kept scrupulously clean. Treatment for shock.
Third-degree	Damage to all layers of skin. Shock.	Requires specialist treatment.

Splints

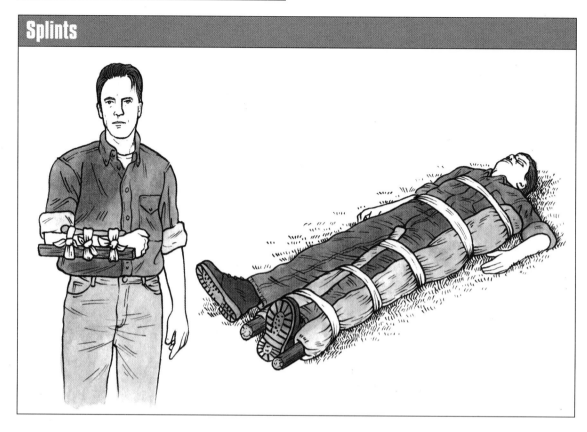

of shock are inevitably worsened by pain and anxiety.

The major signs of shock are:

- Pulse – fast and almost imperceptible.
- Pallor – pale skin; cold, clammy; sweating; shivering.
- Pupils – dilated.

Treatment for shock

- ABC – Airways, Breathing, Circulation.
- Lie victim down and elevate legs.
- Provide moderate warmth.
- Loosen tight clothing.
- Provide reassurance.
- Control the bleeding.
- Replace fluid intravenously. Do not give the victim food or drink.
- Provide pain relief if possible.
- Call for medical assistance and/or evacuate by stretcher.

FRACTURE

This is a break in a bone, usually caused by a fall. A closed, or simple, fracture is where the broken bone ends remain beneath the skin, whereas an open, or compound, fracture is where both ends of the bone protrude through the skin.

Signs

Swelling, deformity or projecting bone ends. Severe pain, made worse by movement.

Treatment

- Do not try to force the bones back together again but seek medical assistance.
- Treat all open wounds with a clean dressing.
- Splint the fractured area in exactly the position that you find it in, pending removal to hospital or the arrival of expert medical aid.

Emergency sling

- If the arm is fractured, splint it, and then set up a sling if the arm can be moved across the chest.
- Do not move the victim at all if you suspect a spinal injury.

Splints

You can use sticks, tree branches, boards or even a rolled newspaper to make a splint. The splint should be long enough to immo- bilise the limb above and below the fracture. Ensure the limb and splint are tied at four points, two above and two below the frac- ture. Tie the splint with non-slip knots, with the knot on the outside.

Make sure that the splint is adequately padded anywhere it touches a bony part of the body, otherwise it will be uncomfortable for the victim. You may tie the wounded limb to another part of the victim's body, e.g. a wounded leg tied to a healthy leg, or a wounded arm to the chest. Place a splint on each side of the limb. When tying the splints on, make sure the bandages are tight enough to prevent the splints from slipping, but not so tight as to impede circulation.

Circulation

It is important to check the circulation below the point of injury before tying on the splints. If there is no circulation in this area for too long, the limb may have to be amputated.

If the skin is pale or bluish in colour, this may indicate damage to an artery. You can also check by pressing down fingernails into the skin and watching how quickly the colour returns (known as capillary return). Check this by comparing with an uninjured extremity. Also check the temperature of the limb against another limb. Check for circula- tion after tying on the splints. Damaged arter- ies require urgent medical attention.

Sling

This can be made from non-stretching cloth or even a belt. The sling should place pres- sure on the uninjured side of the body and the hand should be slightly higher than the elbow when put in place across the body.

Neck fracture

The neck should be immobilised with a cer- vical collar. Alternatively, place a rolled towel or cloth under the neck to support it and two weighted objects on either side of the head to keep it stable until help arrives.

Neck fracture emergency sling

Fractured ribs

A fractured rib causes severe pain, which is worsened by deep breathing. Strapping is rarely used for a rib injury because of the difficulty of maintaining breathing with a strap in place. The victim should be encouraged to hold the injured side while taking deep breaths. There is a danger that a fractured rib might pierce a lung. The signs of this may include difficulty in breathing, a blue colour (cyanosis) and shock. Get urgent medical help.

Skull fracture

Most skull fractures are closed and do not create complications. A severe injury may cause bone fragments to be forced inwards, rupturing the blood vessels of the membrane covering the brain. The blood clot that results may press on to brain tissue.

If there is straw-coloured fluid seeping from an ear or the nose, this may indicate rupture of the brain membrane blood vessels by a fracture of the base of the skull. The victim should be put in the recovery position, allowing any fluid to run out. Call for urgent medical assistance.

DISLOCATION

Dislocation means the displacement of two bones in a joint, and usually involves tearing the joint ligament and damage to the joint capsule. A fracture can also be involved. Symptoms are severe pain and swelling round the joint. Do not attempt to manipulate the bones back into position unless you have had First Aid training. Instead, make a splint or, if it is a dislocated shoulder, a sling in order to prevent movement. Call for medical assistance.

If you have First Aid training, act quickly before the muscles around the joint begin to tighten up. Apply traction or pull the joint, then move the attached limb in the direction that it would normally move. Release the traction or pulling force and check for nerve response. If a nerve is pinched, repeat the procedure. Apply cold packs to reduce the swelling.

SPRAIN

Sprain is the tearing or stretching of the ligaments in a joint caused by a sudden strain. It usually applies to the ankle, when the complete weight of the body is placed on the ankle by a falling motion towards the outside of the foot. There is usually pain and a spasm or contraction of the muscles round the joint.

Apply an ice pack (if available; alternatively a container filled with cold spring water) to the area of the sprain. Bandage with a compression bandage, and raise the injured part. Take pain-relieving drugs if necessary.

If for any reason the victim needs to keep walking, they should keep on their footwear. It can act partially as a splint, and will be difficult to put back on if removed.

SLINGS AND BANDAGES

Arm sling

The wrist should be slightly higher than the elbow. Place an open triangular bandage between the body and the arm with one point towards the elbow. Take the upper point over the shoulder on the uninjured side and round the neck. Bring the lower point under, then up and over, the arm and tie it to the upper point with a reef knot. Fold any excess bandage over the elbow and secure it with a safety pin.

St John sling

The elbow should be beside the body and the hand extended towards the uninjured shoulder.

Place an open triangular bandage over the forearm and hand with the point towards the elbow.

Extend the upper point of the bandage over the uninjured shoulder. Tuck the lower part of the bandage under the injured arm, bring it under the elbow and round the back and extend the lower point up to meet the

Arm sling

upper point at the shoulder. Tie it with a reef knot. Fold the excess material and use a safety pin. Make sure that the sling is tucked under the arm and that it gives firm support.

Collar and cuff
Allow the elbow to hang at the side and place the hand extended towards the shoulder on the uninjured side. Tie a clove hitch

with two loops, one towards you and one away from you. Put the loops together by sliding your hands under the loops and closing with a clapping motion. Then tie a clove hitch directly on the wrist. Slide the clove hitch over the hand and gently pull it firmly to secure the wrist. Extend the points of the bandage to either side of the neck and tie firmly with a reef knot.

St John sling

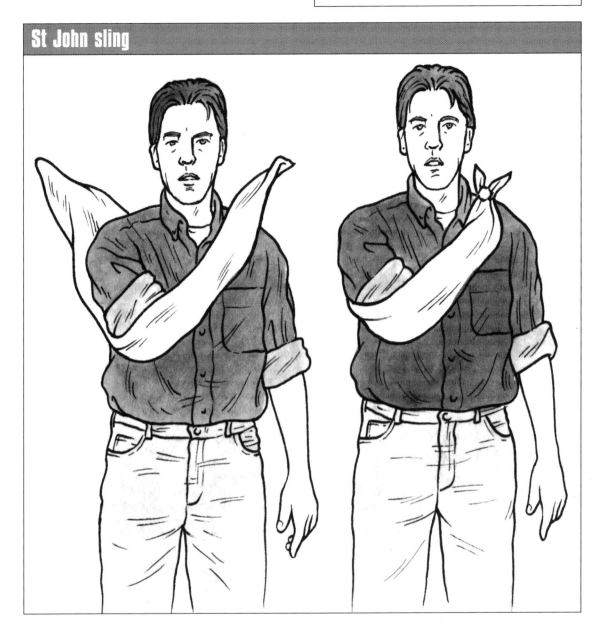

Leg bandage

Place the centre of the triangular bandage over the dressing of the wound. Take the lower end round and up the leg in a spiral motion and the upper end round and down the leg in a spiral motion, overlapping slightly on each turn. Bring both ends together and tie them with a non-slip knot.

Foot bandage

Place the foot in the middle of the triangular bandage with the heel well forward of the base. Make sure the toes are separated with absorbent material to prevent chafing and irritation of the skin. Place the forward point over the top of the foot and tuck any excess material into the pleats on each side of the foot. Cross the ends on top of the foot, take them round the ankle and tie them at the front of the ankle.

Hand bandage

Put the hand on the bandage with the wrist at the base of the bandage. Fingers can be separated with soft material to prevent them chafing. Bring the apex of the bandage up and over the fingers and then bring the ends round to tie them at the wrist.

POISONOUS BITES OR STINGS

Snake bite

If the bite is on an arm or leg, place a constricting band, of one to two finger lengths, above and below the bite. If you only have one band, place it between the bite and the victim's heart. The band should be tight enough to prevent the flow of blood near the skin of the affected area, but not tight enough to interfere with circulation. If available, place an ice bag over the area of the bite. Do not attempt to suck out the venom. Do not use ointments on the bite. Do not give the victim food, coffee or tea, drugs or tobacco.

Insect bites and stings

Remove the stinger by scraping the flesh. Do not squeeze the sack attached to the stinger. Wash the area with soap and water. Use an ice pack on the area if available as this will reduce the spread of poison. If the reaction to the bite or sting is serious, treat as for snake bite.

Hand bandage

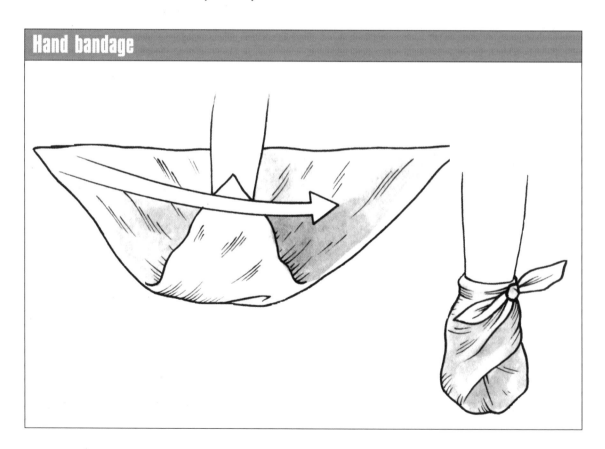

Stings from spiny fish, urchins, stingrays and cone shells

Soak the wound in hot water for between 30 and 60 minutes. This will help to deactivate the toxin, which is heat-sensitive.

Animal bites

Clean the wound thoroughly, flushing it out with water. Cover the wound with a sterile dressing. If an arm or leg is injured, immobilise it. Find medical help as soon as possible. Try to provide as much information as possible about the animal so that the appropriate treatment can be given.

Ingestion of poisonous berries or tablets

If it is certain that poisonous berries or tablets have been eaten, you can induce vomiting by turning the victim on their side and forcing two fingers down to the back of the throat.

Worms

Ways of preventing worms and other intestinal parasites are to avoid going barefoot, to avoid uncooked meat and raw vegetables that have come into contact with human waste, and to observe good habits of cleanliness such as washing daily. If you do not carry a worm medicine, try one of the following:

Salt water

Dissolve four tablespoons in 2US/1¾UK pints (1 litre) of water. Use this method only once.

Tobacco

Eat one or one and a half cigarettes. Do not repeat the treatment for at least 24 hours.

Kerosene

Take a dose of two tablespoons, taking care not to inhale the fumes. Again, do not repeat the dose for at least 24 hours.

Hot peppers

Eaten as part of your daily diet, hot peppers will successfully keep parasites at bay.

HEAT INJURIES

The availability of water, shelter and wearing the correct kind of clothing are crucial factors in the control of heat injuries (see Chapter 2, Survival in the Desert).

A balance must be kept between sweating (which keeps the body cool) and the intake of water. If heavy work is to be carried out, the quantity of water intake must rise to compensate. As well as exertion, other factors that can affect susceptibility to heat injury are weight, health, fitness and food, and alcohol intake.

Heat cramps

They are caused by too many body salts being lost, for example, by excessive sweating, vomiting or diarrhoea. Signs of heat cramps include cramps in the arms, legs or abdomen, heavy sweating and thirst. Move the victim to a cool, shady area, give him/her water to drink, and loosen clothing. Seek medical assistance if there is no improvement.

Heat exhaustion

This is caused by an imbalance between sweating and water intake. The major signs of heat exhaustion include heavy sweating with a pale, clammy skin; headache; dizziness and confusion.

Move the victim to a cool, shady area, give him/her water to drink, and loosen clothing. The victim should not be under exertion for the rest of the day. Seek medical assistance if the symptoms do not disappear.

Heatstroke

This is caused by a failure of the body's cooling mechanisms after prolonged exposure to heat and sun. The lack of sweat causes the skin to become red and dry. The victim may have a rapid, weak pulse, headache, dizziness and nausea.

Move the victim urgently to a cool, shaded area. Give him/her water to drink slowly if conscious, and cool down the victim with water externally, if there is enough available. Massage the victim's extremities to improve the blood flow and raise their legs.

Seek medical assistance immediately and monitor the victim carefully in case further First Aid is required, such as ABC.

COLD INJURIES

The susceptibility to cold injuries can be aggravated by wind, water, anxiety, dehydration, lack of food, physical condition, physical type, lack of rest, and by psychological factors such as depression, anxiety and poor leadership.

To prevent cold injury, wear layers of clothing that can be adapted to the changes of temperature and amount of exertion. Do not wear so many clothes as to cause sweat, as this will lead to both dehydration and wet clothing, which in turn will lose its heat retentiveness. Have warm clothing, such as a woollen pullover, to put on when you have stopped walking, for example.

Cold injuries can be difficult to detect, especially by the person who is suffering. Tingling or pins and needles can be signs of a cold injury, as can be pale skin in the area of the injury. Slight cold injury can be treated by placing the affected part in warmth, such as placing cold feet in a warm dry area where circulation can begin to improve. Do not expose the affected part to direct heat or attempt to massage. Deep cold injury requires urgent treatment and medical assistance.

Chilblains

This is caused by lengthy exposure of the skin to low temperatures which causes constriction of the small blood vessels that lie below the surface of the skin. Chilblains presents itself as an itchy, purple-red swelling, usually on a toe or finger. The symptoms should disappear as soon as the affected part is warmed, e.g. exposed hands put in warm gloves.

Trench foot or immersion foot

This is caused by the exposure of feet to wet and damp conditions over a prolonged period. Feet will initially turn pale, with little detectable pulse, and later become red, swollen and painful, with a strong pulse. If the feet are at the stage where they are pale, warm them gently. Do not expose them to direct heat as this can lead to gangrene (tissue death).

If the feet are at the stage where they are red and swollen, cool them down gradually. Painkillers may be required. Do not massage the feet or apply direct heat or cold, such as ice. To prevent trench foot, ensure that socks are changed daily. You can keep up a rota of socks by tying a damp pair round your midriff where they will dry as you go about your activities.

Frostbite

Direct exposure to wind and cold can cause frostbite by damaging tissue. The symptoms are pins and needles followed by numbness. The skin is first white, cold and hard, then it becomes red and swollen. There is a danger of gangrene if the blood vessels are affected. Place the victim in a warm area and remove clothing from the affected part. Put clean, warm clothing on the affected part and keep in a warm area, such as under the armpits if it is your own hand. Seek medical assistance.

Hypothermia

Hypothermia involves body temperature falling *below* 99°F (37°C). The signs are drowsiness and lowered breathing and heart rate, which can lead to unconsciousness and even death. Wind chill and wet clothing can increase the susceptibility to hypothermia.

Treatment involves urgent rewarming of the whole body, evenly and gently. If the victim has any wet or frozen clothing, remove it and replace it with clean dry clothing. Place the victim in a sleeping bag in a warm protected area. Ideally someone else should also be in the sleeping bag to improve the warming conditions. Be ready to give artificial respiration if the victim's breathing stops. Seek medical assistance immediately.

PSYCHOLOGICAL FACTORS

Anxiety

This is a sense of impending disaster, which can be brought on in a survival environment by the difficulties of finding basic needs. Symptoms may include palpitations, stabbing pains in the chest and difficulty in breathing, sighing and overbreathing. There may also be muscle tension, pains in the back and a tendency to grasp things too tightly. Other symptoms may include dry mouth, diarrhoea, nausea, belching and difficulty in swallowing. External symptoms may include pallor, sweating and yawning.

Anxiety will reduce performance if steps are not taken to counter it. The best short-term way of coping is to try to identify the particular problems causing the anxiety. Write them down and deal with them one by one. As you deal with the problems that are making you anxious, you are likely to become more confident and less anxious.

Depression

Depression can involve a feeling of hopelessness or inability to cope, perhaps in the face of overwhelming difficulties or repeated failure. Anxiety can be linked to depression, and in many people the symptoms involve slowing down and listlessness.

Depression can be made worse by feelings of guilt or personal fault, especially where there is little reassurance to the con-

trary. A depressed person may feel that anyone else would have performed better in particular circumstances. This may result from over-competitive or dominating behaviour by others. A cure for this negative way of thinking is for the depressed person to think about and develop their personal gifts and to take sensible measures in dealing with weaknesses.

Depression is common and should be viewed as something that will pass away. Consider that even a great man like Winston Churchill suffered from depression, which he called his 'black dog', but he did not allow it to grip him for too long. Try and view your depression dispassionately and do not let it grow roots. Let it pass away.

Stress

It will be natural to suffer stress in a survival environment, especially one that has involved any kind of accident. Stress is the body's natural way of dealing with problems that require urgent reactions, and in the right circumstances it will improve performance. If the stress factor continues for a long period, however, the body's reactions have a tiring effect which actually reduces the ability of the individual to cope. Exposure to stressful situations can cause symptoms of anxiety or depression, such as palpitations, indigestion and muscular aches and pains.

The best way to deal with stress is to attempt to control it. Your ability to control it will improve with practice, though in the early stages there is a strong urge to let the body's reactions rule you and for you to lose your composure. When circumstances allow, make a conscious effort to calm your racing mind and to slow your physical movements (unless of course you are in an emergency, such as a fire, where you need to think and move very fast). Identify the problems that are stressing you, itemise them and set about dealing with them one by one.

CHAPTER NINE

Firemaking, Tools and Weapons

Survival is, in essence, about making the best use of available resources so that what is lacking can be made useful, and what is available can be used in the most efficient way.

Fire has long been one of the fundamental tools of mankind, giving him superiority over other animals and which gave him a multitude of options in mastering his environment. From Neolithic times, man learned how to create fire by creating friction with tools, such as saws and drills and by producing sparks with stones such as flint.

Firemaking

Whichever area you find yourself in, whether it be deserts, tropics or polar regions, a fire is always essential. A fire will provide warmth and dry clothes, it will cook food and heat drinks, it will keep wild animals at bay and ward off insects. It provides light, it can be used for signalling and, last but not least, a fire provides a special morale booster.

In order to start and maintain a successful fire it is vital to collect the right grades of material and to get the balance right between the different elements of the fire, which are air, heat and fuel.

Materials
Tinder
This is required to get a fire started from the first sparks and may consist of wood shavings, lining of bark, sawdust, cotton fluff, bird down, dried grass or pine needles.

Kindling
This is the material you use to expand the fire to the stage when it can take larger fuel. It includes twigs, bark, tufts of dry grass, paper or rags soaked in fuel.

Fuel
This may be wood, such as dead branches or the inside of trees, coal, peat (as long as it is dry enough – look at the top of undercut banks), dry animal dung, or dry grasses twisted into bunches.

Site
Build the fire in a place where it will not be put out by a strong wind or falling snow, or where it is likely to set light to vegetation or your equipment. Consider whether you will need to build stones round the fire to concentrate the heat (for cooking), or whether you

will need to construct a reflector to maximise the heat in a shelter.

The fire should be built on a firm base, which can be made up of stones, green wood or solid earth (this may involve digging down). The fire may need to be in a hole in the ground or surrounded by rocks if wind is likely to be a problem.

TYPES OF FIRES
There are a number of different kinds of fire lays that are suitable for different uses and areas.

Safety night fire
This type of fire is designed to burn through the night with minimal risk of falling logs. It can also include a heat reflector, set back from the fire. It is designed to have few air spaces, so that the flame will burn low, and two leaning logs have the effect of pushing the fire away from your shelter.

Safety night fire

Long fire

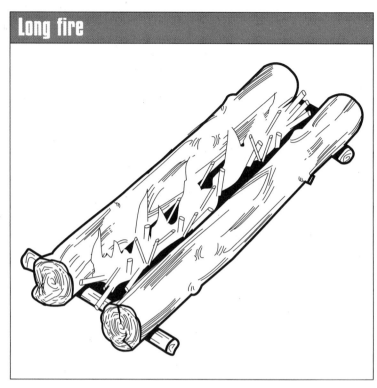

Long fire

This fire can be constructed either as a trench or between two parallel green logs. The logs should be thick, and may be supported by two sticks to improve the airflow.

T-fire

Just as it sounds, this is a fire kindled in a simple T shape carved out in the earth. It is an ideal fire lay for cooking on, since the main fire can be maintained in the top part of the T, while cooking can be done on hot coals and embers that fall into the stem of the T.

Tepee fire

This fire is good for both

cooking and heat, and is constructed with a slanting stick fixed into the ground over some tinder. Other sticks are then leant on the slanting stick, leaving a suitable opening on the wind side. The fire should be lit with your back to the wind.

Star fire

An economical fire which should be made with hardwood logs. The logs are arranged in a star shape and gradually pushed inwards as they burn away.

Pyramid fire

Lay two logs parallel to each other, and lay a number of smaller logs across them to

Tepee fire

Pyramid fire

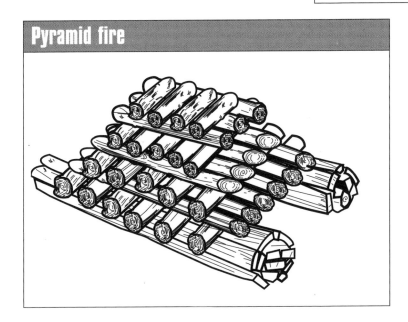

travelling to set up other means of fire lighting.

Magnifying glass

Again, you should carry a magnifying glass in your survival kit, and its advantage over matches is that it will not wear out. Angle the glass to obtain a concentrated ray of heat on to some dry tinder, which should start smoking and then glow red. Blow gently to encourage a flame.

Flint

In your survival kit you should have a fire-lighting

form a base. Lay another layer of yet smaller logs at right angles to form the next layer, and so on, until you have a small layer at the top on which to light your tinder. The fire will gradually burn downwards, making it a good long-term fire to have during the night.

LIGHTING A FIRE

Make sure you gather all materials before you start.

Matches

Windproof matches are the easiest and most obvious way of lighting a fire, and you should have a set in your survival kit. You might, however, wish to keep these for emergencies or you may have run out. If you are planning to set out on a journey, keep the matches, since you will have less time when

Star fire

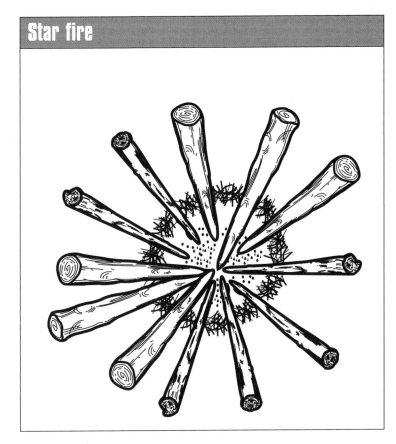

Bow and drill

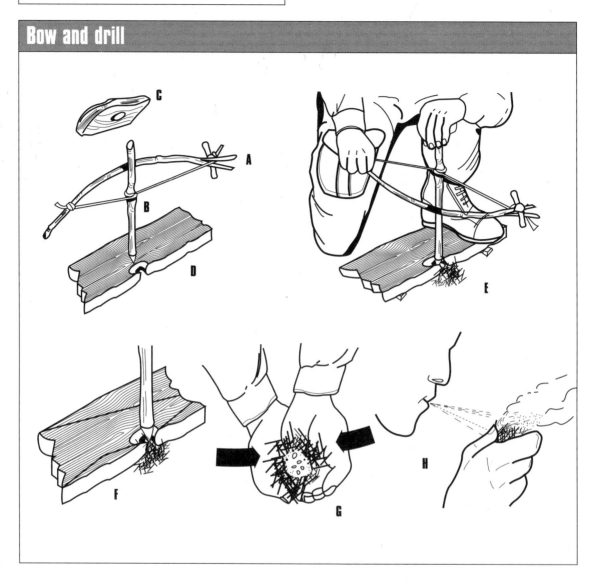

piece of equipment which consists of a small saw and a small metal bar. It is easy to draw the saw across the bar to produce a strong spark. Otherwise, a piece of flintstone can be struck with metal to produce the same effect.

Battery

You can attach wires to each terminal of the battery and touch the wires together to produce a spark.

Gunpowder

You can carefully remove a bullet from a round and use its gunpowder to start a fire.

Bow and drill

Make the bow from a piece of willow with a string stretched across it, end to end (A). The drill should be a single shaft of dry wood with one end pointed and the other rounded (B). The rounded end should fit into a hole hollowed out of a fist-sized piece of wood (C),

Fire plough

Hardwood

Softwood

which is used to hold the drill vertical in the hand. The pointed end goes downwards into a notch in a piece of wood below which is tinder (D). Move the bow in a regular way back and forth so that the string turns the drill (E). With increasing pressure and speed, it creates the friction in the lower block of wood that will eventually produce smoke and light the tinder (F). Remove the bow and spindle and place the tinder placed next to the glowing ember (G). Roll tinder around the burning ember and blow to burn the tinder (H).

Hand drill
This is a similar method to the bow and drill, but without the bow. Rub a piece of hollow softwood between your hands, running them down the shaft as you go. The effect will be similar to that described above.

Fire plough
Cut a groove into a softwood base and then use a hardwood stick to plough up and down it. Small particles of wood are thrown up by the ploughing and the friction should eventually ignite them.

TOOLS AND WEAPONS

Club
The club is a basic and useful tool which can be used

Bow and arrows

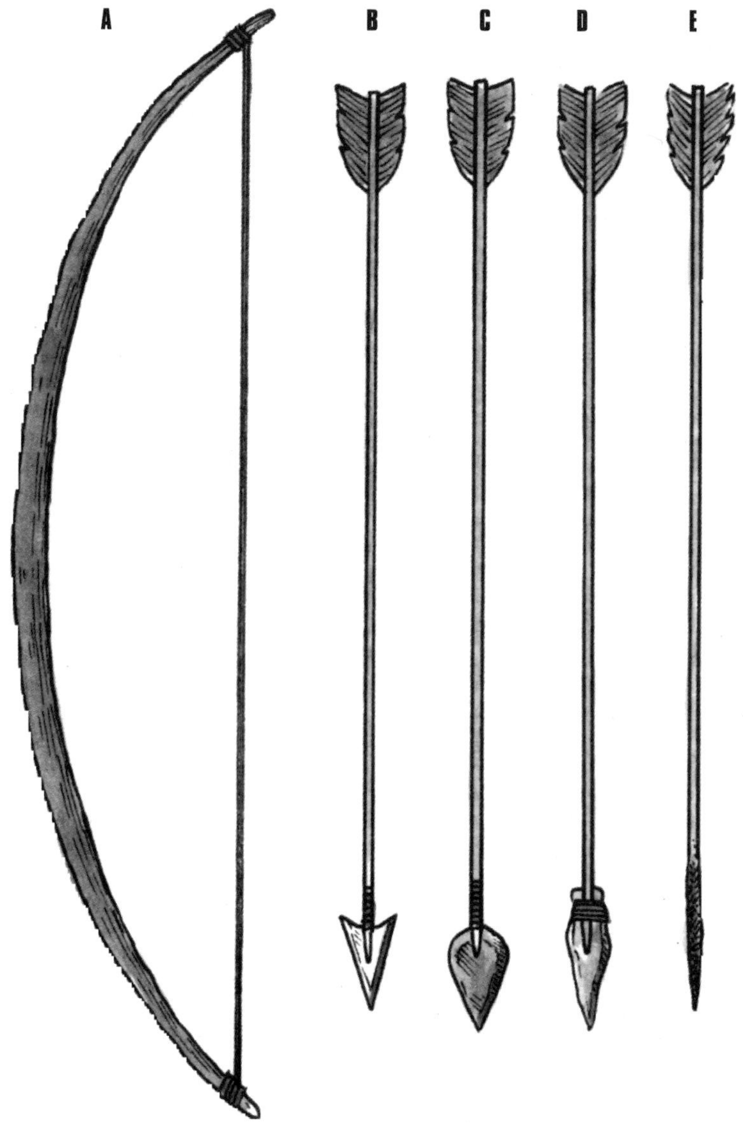

A Hardwood and rawhide

B Tin arrowhead

C Flint arrowhead

D Bone arrowhead

E Burnt-wood arrowhead

for finishing off animals caught in traps, or for killing slow-moving animals, as well as for providing a sense of security.

The easiest club to make is a medium-sized staff which is thick at one end and fits securely into the hand. It may be that you will find a piece of wood that fits the requirement; otherwise you can fashion one with your knife.

Other types of club can be made in the stone-age manner. Take a forked stick and fit a slightly narrower stone into the fork, and lash the fork ends securely. Alternatively, the end of the wood can be shaved and bent over the stone, to be lashed back onto the shaft. This kind of club will require careful construction and maintenance.

Throwing stick

Find a piece of hardwood bent naturally at about 45° and shape it like a boomerang. If you cannot find a curved stick, use a straight one about 2ft (60cm) long with a thickened end.

Spear

The simplest kind of spear is a bamboo shaft shaved on one side at the end. This will provide a very sharp and useful weapon that can be used on small game. Similar spears can be made from hardwood poles sharpened at the end. Alternatively, attach a piece of sharp metal or bone to the end of a shaft by splitting the shaft at the end and inserting the blade into the groove before lashing it securely.

A prong-like effect can also be achieved by splitting the end of the shaft and keeping the sharp points apart with spacers lashed in. This kind of spear will be useful for fishing.

Bow and arrow

This classic hunting equipment should be constructed with some care, and with the knowledge that it will have a limited lifespan due to lack of seasoned wood. Try to use a hardwood stick and fashion it in such a way that it is evenly weighted at both ends, taking advantage of any natural bend in the wood.

A stick can be shaved on the insides at both ends, away from the central area, which will be gripped in the hand, in order to improve its qualities. Cut notches at both ends for the string, which should ideally be made from rawhide. Sling the bow taut but not too tight.

The wood can be maintained by rubbing animal fat or oil into it. The arrows can be sharpened hardwood sticks or have suitable pieces of stone, bone, metal or glass attached. Ideally, the arrows should have feathers to improve the flight, but it is not strictly necessary. Make a notch at the end of the arrow to fit into the bow string.

Catapult

You will need a Y-shaped stick as well as some elastic material, such as the inner tube of a tyre.

Sling

One piece of material will hold one or more stones. One end of the material is released when the sling is swung in the direction of the prey and released. Practice will be required to achieve accuracy.

Bola

In the manner of the South American gauchos, the bola consists of stones attached to string about 3ft (1m) in length. Three stones should be enough. Swing the stones above your head, taking care not to hit yourself, and release in the direction of the prey. Practice is definitely required if this weapon is not to be of greater danger to yourself than to your prey.

Fishhooks

You can make fishhooks out of any small pieces of sharp material that are likely to be swallowed by a fish when it takes the bait. A gorge can be made out of a small piece of hardwood notched in the middle to take the line and sharp at both ends.

CHAPTER TEN

Trapping, Fishing and Plant Food

There is food available in nature's pantry but obtaining it can require both hard work and skill. You need to be aware also of the dangers presented by certain kinds of plants and animals.

TRAPPING

It is important to have a good idea of the size of the animal you wish to trap as well as to find out where its runs and trails are. This can be determined by looking for droppings, tracks, burrows, hair and fur.

The difference between an animal trail and a run is that the former will be used by a variety of animals, whereas the latter is used by only one species. Make sure your trap is adapted to the run and to the animal you wish to catch.

Positioning snares

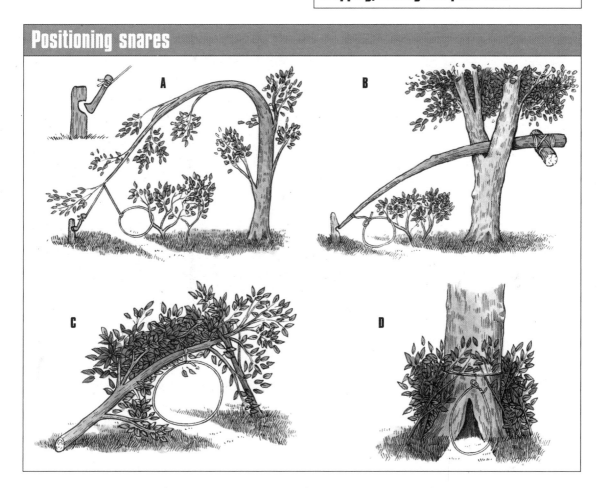

Snares

A snare is a wire or string loop placed in such a way that an animal is forced to put its head through it. The snare then tightens, killing the animal, though not always immediately. Commercial snares are often self-locking, but the home-made variety can be just as effective. You should have some simple snares in your survival kit and try to disguise your human smell on the snare by smearing your hand with mud when handling it, and/or covering the snare with ashes.

Positioning Snares

Position the snare in such a way in the animal's run that it will be difficult for the animal to avoid it. Keep the loop open and unre-stricted, and a proper distance off the ground. Wire snares are easy to position because of their rigidity.

Set snares on heavily used trails or in areas where animals feed on vegetation or a carcass (A, B and C), or near a den or frequently visited food store (D). Do not place the snare too near water, as the animal will be extra alert in these areas. Arrange the surrounding vegetation in such a way that there is a tunnel just before the snare, slightly wider than the animal's body. Take care to avoid breaking vegetation when setting up the channel and leave the area looking as natural as possible, by, for example, smearing mud into cuts in trees.

The snare will need to be attached to a firmly embedded stick or branch that will hold the animal when it struggles. Make sure you regularly check any snares you have set up, since the animal will have a better chance of escaping given more time, and it may also be taken by another predator. Animals will normally be moving about at first and last lights.

Twitch-up snare

This type of snare will release a branch under tension or with a counterweight. Use two forked sticks, one with a short fork to act as a catch. One stick is driven into the ground, while the other is attached to cord holding a sapling under tension. This device should be set up in such a way that when the animal runs through the snare it pulls the fork attached to the sapling away from the catch.

An alternative method is to set two sticks with notches in them into the ground on either side of the run. Attach one end of a cord to the sapling and tie the other end to a cross bar which should be set into the notches. The crossbar should be high enough not to impede the run of the animal, and the open snare should be set below it.

Traps
Deadfall

Deadfalls are activated either by trip wires or by bait. If the animal runs through a wire or takes the bait, a weight such as a heavy log, branch or stone falls on it and traps or kills it.

Making a figure four trigger

A figure four trigger consists of an upright stick, a release stick and a bait stick. For the upright stick, cut the top at an angle and square off the tip to allow it to fit into a notch in the release stick. Cut a square notch near the bottom to fit a corresponding square notch in the bait stick. Flatten the sides of the stick at this notch to guarantee a good fit.

For the release stick, cut the top so the deadfall will rest on it securely until triggered. Cut a notch near the top in which to

fit the upright stick. Then, cut the bottom end at an angle to fit into the bait stick.

To make the bait stick, cut a notch near one end in which to place the end of the release stick. Shape the other end to hold the bait and cut a square notch at the spot where it crosses the upright stick. The notches in the upright stick and the bait should fit firmly together.

Rest the trigger on a stone or a piece of wood to stop it sinking into the ground.

N.B. Deadfall traps are easily set off and can kill humans. Always remember where you have set your traps.

Spear trap

With this device a branch is held under tension with one or more sharp spears attached to it. When the animal trips the wire, the spring-loaded branch is released which drives the spear into the animal. Great care must be taken when setting or checking these traps so that they are not set off inadvertently. Always approach from behind the spear point.

N.B. Spear traps can kill. Always make sure that you approach them from behind.

Bird trap

A bird trap can consist simply of nooses suspended over a branch where birds alight.

ANIMAL HAZARDS

- Do not tackle animals such as bears, wolves, big cats, crocodiles, alligators and poisonous snakes, unless you feel it is absolutely necessary.
- Do not put yourself in a position where you are cornering a dangerous animal by blocking its escape route.
- Beware all animals that are still alive in traps. They will fight for their lives and deliver severe bites.
- If you find yourself confronted by a

Deadfall traps

A figure four trigger, effective and easy to make

A deadfall with a baited release trigger

A deadfall with a tripline release trigger

A deadfall /snare combination

A trigger for a deadfall /snare combination

Spear traps

Ensure the spear is lashed securely to the springy shaft. If not it may be knocked sideways on inpact

dangerous animal, breathe deeply to control your nerves and to convey confidence to the animal. Talk calmly and move away slowly and with assurance.

- Make sure a large animal is dead before getting too close. Test by stabbing it with a spear or knife on a stick before you come near it.

FISHING

Fish are an excellent source of protein and can be caught in a variety of ways. Fish tend to be attracted to the shaded parts of streams and to deep pools and backwaters.

Bait

Bait should be as similar as possible to what the fish in the area are already feeding on, for example worms, insects, minnows, maggots or scraps of flesh.

Fish traps

You can construct traps, such as fish baskets, made of several sticks lashed together to form a funnel pointing into the basket with a bait. The fish should be able to swim in but not out again.

A similar trap can be made out of a bottle, where the bottom of the bottle is broken

Fish lines

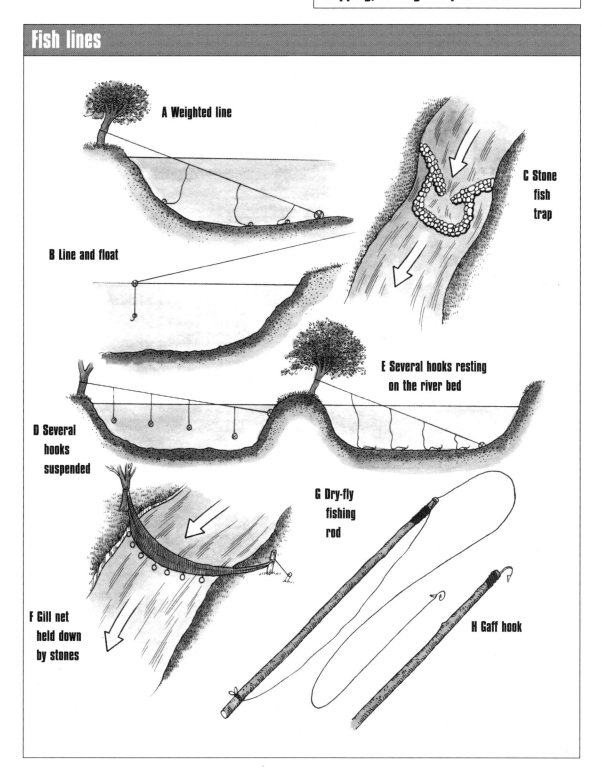

A Weighted line

C Stone fish trap

B Line and float

E Several hooks resting on the river bed

D Several hooks suspended

G Dry-fly fishing rod

F Gill net held down by stones

H Gaff hook

Fish basket

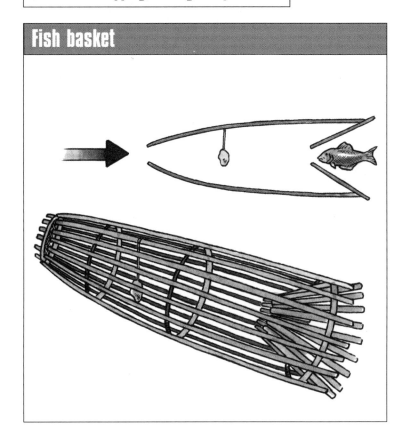

struggle on the surface of the water and attract the attention of fish.

Nets

You can narrow a stream with stones in order to channel fish to where a net is placed at one end of the stream. Ensure the net is held securely so that it is not taken away by the fish or any other floating material. Nets can be strung out across a stream with stones to weigh down the bottom of the net.

Spearfishing

You will need to be near shallow water where the fish are large and plentiful. You can use a piece of sharpened bamboo as a spear, or a sharpened sapling, or a pole with a knife, or other blade, attached to the end.

and jagged where it funnels inward. Or, cut a plastic bottle off at the head, then turn the head round and insert it into the bottle.

Put the end of your spear under water and move it slowly towards the fish. Then impale a fish with a sharp strike. If you are successful, it is probably best not to try and lift the fish onto the bank with the spear, but reach down and grab the fish with your free hand.

Line fishing

You can leave lines out in a river with weights attached and smaller lines trailing off them. This gives you a better chance of getting a catch. You can check the lines for a catch occasionally.

Fly fishing

A fishing rod can be improvised from a suitable branch with a line and fly attached. The fly should be whisked on to the surface of the water upstream and allowed to float downstream. Fish will only attempt a bite during seasons when flies and insects are at large. You can use something like a beetle or grasshopper for this kind of fishing, as it will

STALKING PREY

- If you are going to stalk animals, make sure you have not used any strong soaps or other scent, and wash yourself in clean water to remove other smells.
- You can help to mask your smell by standing in the smoke of a fire for a while.
- When hunting, move against the wind and start out at first light.
- Do not take long strides, but remain balanced. Move carefully, rolling the foot from the heel through to the toes on each

Gutting animals

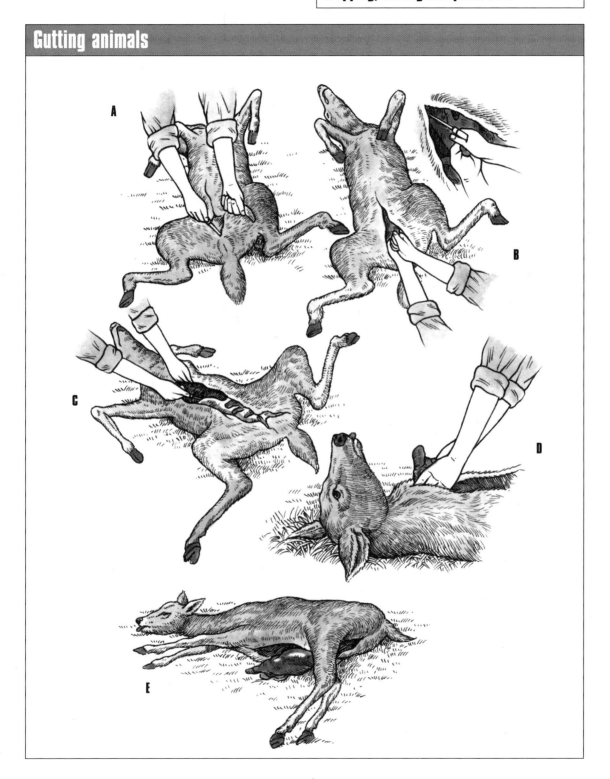

Filleting fish

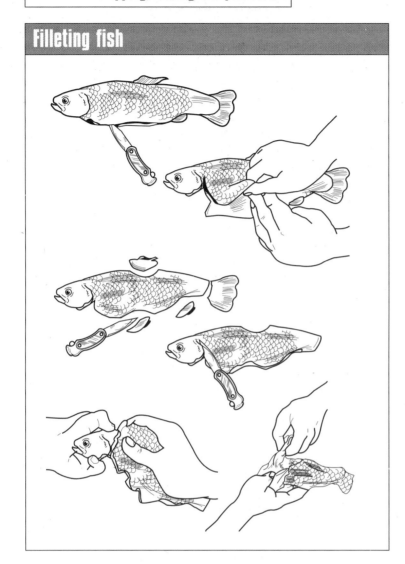

PREPARING FOOD

When an animal is caught it needs to be gutted and skinned properly if it is not to cause unpleasant side effects when eaten.

Gutting

First drain the blood by slitting the throat. Cut around the anus and cut the skin parallel to the penis if the animal is male (A). Insert two fingers between the skin and the membrane containing the entrails. Place the knife blade between your two fingers and cut up towards the chin (B). Cut the diaphragm at the rib cage, and cut the pelvic bone and remove the anus (C). Split open the breast and remove as much of the windpipe as possible (D). Turn the animal on its side and roll out the entrails (E).

If it is a large animal, you will need to cut it up to make it manageable. You can cut through the tissue connecting the front legs to the body and cut the hindquarters off. Cut away the muscles on either side of the spine and separate the ribs from the backbone. You can either cook large pieces of meat over a spit or boil them. Boil or stew smaller pieces.

step, so that you can feel for breakable twigs, and other things likely to make a noise, under your feet.

- Crawl on hands and knees when necessary to avoid being seen by alert animals.
- Stop moving when an animal looks in your direction. Move again when it resumes feeding.
- If you get within range, aim at a point just behind the front shoulder.
- Do not immediately chase a wounded, bolting animal but give it time to stop again.

Skinning

It is easier to skin an animal immediately after killing, and it may be easier to remove the entrails after it has been skinned.

Slit the skin from anus to neck, taking care to cut round the anus (A-B-C). Cut up the inside of the leg to the knee joint. Cut round the legs at the joint. Beginning at the rear legs, peel the skin away until you reach the back, and then remove the skin downwards towards the head. Take the skin off by cutting round the neck.

Curing

A rough way of curing the skin is to wash it to remove blood and fleas and scrape the inner side of the skin using a stone and sand or earth.

Birds

Remove feathers by plucking or skinning. Open up the body and remove entrails, except the craw, heart and liver. Cut off the feet.

Filleting fish

Slit from the anus to behind the gills and pull out the internal organs. Wash and clean the flesh and cut off the fins and tail. Cut down to the spine, but not through it. Cut round the spine, finishing behind the gills on both sides. Insert your thumb along the top of the spine and pull it away from the flesh. The ribs should come away with the spine.

Cooking methods

Boiling

Ideally, this should be done in a metal container, such as a can, but you can also boil water in a bamboo stem if it is slanted over the fire.

Roasting

The meat should be skewered on a spit and turned over hot embers. Ensure the meat does not cook too quickly on the outside without cooking the inside.

Baking

You can either use some form of metal container as an oven or improvise by digging a pit under a fire.

Frying

Place food on a flat piece of rock on a fire.

Food tips

Insects and worms

Boil, or dry and crush before adding to soups and stews.

Shellfish

Boil as soon as possible to prevent them going off and to destroy harmful organisms.

Turtles and tortoises

Boil until the shell comes off. Cut meat and cook.

Reptiles

Gut and cook in their skins in hot embers. When the skin splits, remove and boil. Cut off snake heads before cooking. Skin frogs and roast on a stick.

Birds

Boil all carrion. Roast young birds.

Fish

Stew or wrap in leaves and bake.

Meat

Cut into cubes and boil. Wild pig is infested with worms and liver fluke. Venison can also contain worms.

PLANT FOOD

In general you should make sure to avoid :
- Any fruit that is overripe or showing any signs of mildew or fungus.
- Any weeds, leaves or seeds with an almond- like scent, which is anindication of cyanide compound.
- All mushrooms unless you are 100 per cent certain they're safe.
- Plants with a three-leaved growth pattern.
- Beans, bulbs or seeds from pods.
- Foliage that looks like parsley, dill, carrot or parsnip.
- Grain heads with pink, purplish or black spurs.

Universal edibility test

(This test does not apply to fungi/mushrooms)

Test one part of the food at a time. Separate the plant into parts – flower, bud, leaf, stem, root. Smell the plant for acid. Fast for eight hours before testing the plant, and during the fast test for contact poisoning on your elbow or wrist. Do not take anything other than water and the tested plant into the mouth during testing.

Choose a small amount of a particular portion of the plant and prepare it the way you want to eat it. First touch a small portion on the outside of your lip to test for a burning sensation or itching. Wait three minutes. If there is no reaction, place the plant on your tongue and wait 15 minutes. If there is no reaction, thoroughly chew a pinch (without swallowing) and again leave for 15 minutes. If you sense no burning, itching or numbing sensations, swallow the food.

Wait eight hours. If there are any ill-effects, induce vomiting (two fingers down the throat) and drink plenty of water. If you suffer no ill effects, eat a quarter of a cup of the same plant prepared the same way. Wait another eight hours, and if all is well, the plant, as prepared, is safe for eating.

NB One part of a plant may be edible and other parts not. If it is edible cooked, it may not be edible raw (re-test raw). Different individuals may react in different ways to the same part of a plant.

Edible plants

You can find lists of edible plants in the relevant chapter categorised by region. The following list is restricted to examples of plants that do not fall clearly into the desert, tropical or polar categories.

Almond

The almond can be found widely across tropical, temperate and arid areas. Similar to the peach tree, the almond is covered by a thick, brown, dry skin. They are highly nutritious, like all nuts.

Arrowroot

Arrowroot

Found in moist areas throughout temperate and tropical zones. It has arrow-shaped leaves. The roots can be boiled as a vegetable.

Asparagus

Found in temperate areas worldwide. In spring, green, finger-like growths accompany fine foliage and red berries. Boil young stems for at least 15 minutes before eating.

Beech

Found in many temperate zones in moist areas. The tree has a light grey bark and dark green leaves. Beechnuts are edible after removing a thin shell.

Blackberry and raspberry

Found throughout temperate regions. They have prickly stems and edible fruits of different colours. The leaves can be boiled to make tea.

Burdock

Found widely in northern temperate zones. There are arrow-shaped leaves and pink flowers with bristly burs. The leaf stalks can be eaten raw or cooked, and the roots boiled.

Carob

Found in the Mediterranean, Middle East and

Burdock

Chufa
Found in many parts of the world in moist areas. The leaves are similar to grass. You can boil or bake the tubers.

Common jujube
Found widely in tropical, sub-tropical, arid and temperate regions. The fruit can be dried, and the pulp produces water.

Crab apple
Found widely in the northern hemisphere and in savannas. The trees can be 3–40ft (1–12m), and have beautiful white and pink blossoms. The wild fruit itself is much smaller than the cultivated apple, and is an excellent survival staple. It can be eaten raw or boiled, or dried and stored.

Cranberry
Found in the cooler parts of the northern hemisphere. It is a ground creeper with red berries. It should be cooked and eaten with added sugar to avoid an astringent taste.

North Africa. The seedpods are known as St John's bread. The young pods are edible raw or boiled. Older pods can be crushed to make a porridge.

Chestnut
Found in temperate and tropical zones. Chestnuts are traditionally roasted in embers, which causes the shell to crack, revealing the delicious and nutritious nut.

Chicory
Can be found in Africa, Asia, Europe and North America. The leaves are like dandelion with a tall stem that can reach almost 6ft (2m). It has light blue flowers. The leaves and roots can be eaten, the latter boiled.

Chicory

Dandelion

Found in open areas in the northern hemisphere. The flower grows close to the ground and has jagged leaves with bright yellow flowers. All parts of the plant are edible. The roots can be boiled and eaten as a vegetable, or roasted and ground as a coffee substitute.

Dandelion

Elderberry

Found in Europe and North America, mostly in moist areas. It has large compound leaves, cream-coloured flowers in clusters and black berries. Some versions have red berries. The fruits are edible, though take care with the rest of the plant as it is violently purgative.

Hazelnut

Found in Europe, North America and Asia, mostly in open areas. The bush has bristly husks round the nut which is good to eat, especially in autumn.

Juniper

Found in Europe, North America, Asia and North Africa. An evergreen tree, it has needle-like leaves and bluish cones. The berries can be eaten raw or the seeds roasted to make a coffee substitute.

Lotus

Yellow-flowered lotus found in North America, and pink-flowered lotus in the Far East and many other parts of the world. The plant is edible either raw or cooked.

Nettle

Ubiquitous plant with furry bristles that cause a sting lasting a few minutes. The nettle can be boiled for around 15 minutes and is nutritious. You can also make nettle tea. The sting from the Australian variety of nettle can be very severe.

Oak

Found in Europe, North and Central America and Asia. It can be either deciduous or evergreen. Tan oaks produce very bitter acorns, which need days to soak. Otherwise acorns can be boiled.

Persimmon

Found in the Far East, Africa and North America. A deciduous tree with oblong leaves, it produces a large berry about the size of an apricot and is extremely astringent until very ripe, when it becomes sweet and palatable.

Pine

Found widely in Europe, Central and South America, North Africa, the Middle East and parts of Asia. It has needle-like leaves and a sticky sap. The pine nuts can be taken out of the cones and shelled to produce tasty soft white nuts.

Reed

Found in temperate regions mostly in wet areas. The tall, coarse grass can be eaten raw or cooked.

Sassafras

Found in northern temperate regions, growing to a height of up to 50ft (15m). It has deciduous leaves and soft yellow wood. You can eat the young twigs and leaves.

Sea o rach

Found mostly in salty areas in the Mediterranean and North Africa. It has small grey leaves and flowers collected in narrow spikes. The leaves can be eaten.

Sorghum

Found widely in warmer areas. Grass that looks like corn and which can grow up to 10ft (3m) tall. It produces seeds on its panicles, or terminal heads. The grains can be eaten any time and provide nutritious food.

Tamarind

Found widely in Africa, Asia and tropical Central and South America. A large tree may grow to be 80ft (24m) tall. It has pale yellow flowers and a tapering fruit consisting of a pod with seeds. Cook the seeds before eating. The pulp round the seeds can be sucked for water or used to make a drink by adding it to water, though another sweetener like honey is advisable.

Reed

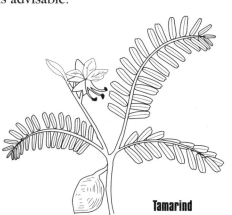

Sorghum

Tamarind

Wild dock

Wild dock and wild sorrel
Found widely in many zones. They are stout plants with small flowers collected in clusters. Eat the leaves either raw or cooked.

Wild rose
Found widely in the northern hemisphere. It is a prickly shrub with red, pink or yellow flowers. You can eat the rose hips when the petals fall. Do not eat the seeds.

POISONOUS PLANTS

Death camas
Deadly poisonous. Found in the United States and eastern Siberia. It has an onion-like appearance, but is distinguished from an onion by not having its familiar smell.

Oleander
Found in Mediterranean and in tropical and temperate regions. Its leaves are leathery and the flowers can range from white to pink, purple or yellow. The sap is highly toxic and is used to make rat poison.

Poison ivy, poison oak, poison sumac
Found throughout the United States and southern Canada. The appearance can vary between shiny and dull-coloured leaves. Leaflets are grouped in threes, and small yellowish or white berries are produced in summer. Its distinguishing characteristics include the regular grouping of three leaflets in each leaf, and stiff clusters of small, yellowish or white berries that appear in summer and autumn. It will cause serious contact dermatitis and severe skin rashes. Keep clear.

Rengbas tree
Found in India and South-East Asia. It has alternating leaves and flowers similar to those of the poison ivy, and again will cause contact dermatitis.

FUNGI
The rule is not to eat a mushroom unless it can be positively identified as 100 per cent safe.

Edible fungi
Chanterelle
Found in coniferous and hardwood forests in midsummer. It has an irregular lobed orange or yellow cap.

Giant puffballs
Grow in grass and shady places from late summer through to autumn. They do not have the usual gills and pores of mushrooms, and are

King boletus

Giant puffballs

creamy white, turning brown with age, when they become unsuitable to eat. Do not eat if the puffball is brown or purplish inside.

King boletus
Found in deciduous woods in summer and early autumn. The cap varies from yellow to greenish as the mushroom gets older.

Oyster mushroom
Grows on rotting tree trunks from midsummer to late autumn. Olive-coloured cap when young, fading with age.

Sulfur mushroom
Appears in the form of a brown wood rot on decaying trees and stumps. It produces bright orange and yellow growths from summer through to autumn. Only eat it when fresh and young.

Shaggy mane
Found widely from spring through to autumn. It has a cylindrical cap covered with shaggy brown scales. Take care of related species that can cause poisoning.

True morels
Found in spring in such places as orchards. The ribbed and pitted cap is greenish yellow or dark olive. Note that there are false morels which should not be eaten.

Truffles
Found underground in areas of Europe. They are whitish when young, becoming darker with age.

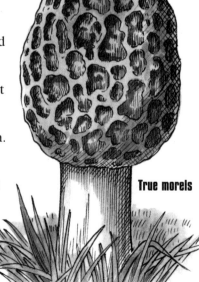

True morels

Poisonous fungi

Potentially poisonous mushrooms number at least 200, and to list them all is beyond the scope of this book. Follow the principle that if you cannot make a positive identification, do not take the risk. Eat something else. A cup-like volva or stem base is a reliable sign of a poisonous mushroom, as are rings round the stem.

Amanita family

Deadly poisonous. These mushrooms contain organic toxins that attack the central nervous system, liver, kidneys and blood vessels. Symptoms may present themselves as much as 12 hours or more after eating the mushroom. Death can follow two or three days later.

Destroying angel

Death cap

Found largely in woods and by the roadside from early summer until late autumn. They have a brightly coloured scaly cap, which can be shades of yellow or orange-yellow. The flesh is yellow beneath the skin, though white deeper down. Gills are white or pale yellow. The stem is white and scaly, and has a characteristic swelling at the volva or base, which has a frill-like ring at the top.

Death cap

Deadly poisonous. Found in woodland from summer through to autumn. It has a greenish-olive cap, a pale stem, white gills and flesh, and a large volva or base.

Destroying angel

Deadly poisonous. Found in woodland in summer and autumn. It is white all over with a scaly stem and large volva. It smells sweet and sickly.

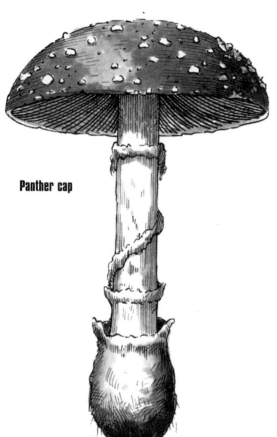

Panther cap

white gills. There are two or three hoop-like rings at the base of the stem.

Leaden entoloma

Deadly poisonous. Found in the summer and autumn, particularly in beech and oak woods. It has a dull white appearance and a convex cap. Gills turn from yellowish to salmon pink. It has no ring on the stem, and smells of radish and bitter almonds.

Fly agaric

Jack-o-lantern

Deadly poisonous, Jack-o-lantern is found at the decayed base of tree stumps and has saffron-yellow gills.

Fly agaric

Dangerously poisonous. Found in pine and birch woods in autumn. It is bright vermilion, fading to orange, and usually flecked with white scales.

Panther cap

Deadly poisonous. Found in woodland, mostly beech. It has a brownish appearance with a white-flecked cap and

CHAPTER ELEVEN

Navigation and Signalling

A vital element of survival is being able to use a map and compass, or other means, to navigate your way to safety and/or being able to signal correctly to potential rescuers.

This chapter provides basic information on using maps and compasses as well as navigating without these usual aids. It is recommended that you make yourself familiar with map reading and navigation techniques before setting out on a major expedition. In the signalling section you will find information on how to attract the attention of rescuers.

Maps

A map uses lines and symbols to portray a certain geographic area, along with its fixed features which can range from mountains and cuttings to footpaths and bars.

Ordnance maps typically have a set of symbols which can be easily understood and which are also explained on the side of the map. Not all maps explain their symbols, so before setting out on a journey into a potentially hazardous environment, make sure that you are familiar with the symbols on the map you are using. In addition to symbols, there will be abbreviations, such as CG – Coastguard.

It is far better to take a reliable and familiar map such as an Ordnance Survey type with you than expect to pick up a map you will be able to understand in the area you are visiting.

Scales

The scale of a map will be represented in either words or figures, such as 1:50,000, which means that one unit of measurement on the map represents 50,000 of the same unit on the ground. The scale line will show equivalent distances, typically in kilometres, miles and nautical miles.

Measuring straight-line distance

The measurement to the right of zero on the map scale is called the primary scale, while the measurement to the left of zero is called the secondary scale. The secondary scale has the primary unit of measurement, e.g. a kilometre, divided into blocks, typically of 10 metres. If you want to measure the distance between two points on the map, mark the points on the edge of a piece of paper. Place the right mark on a point in the primary scale with the left point falling on the secondary scale to measure whatever fraction of a kilometre or mile you wish to acertain.

If you want to measure the distance along a road or track then it is best to use a piece of paper. Place one end at the start and follow the road with the edge of the paper until the road turns away from the paper. Mark the point and swivel the paper round on the pencil until it reaches the road again, and so on.

Grid system

This provides a straightforward and accurate means of finding a position on a map, and it is governed by easily understood rules. The vertical lines on a map are called Eastings and the horizontal lines are called Northings. You always read the Eastings first and the Northings second.

Six-figure grid reference

You read the first half of a printed grid reference along the horizontal grid line, representing Eastings. The last figure of that half will represent tenths of the grid square, so estimate the appropriate distance across the

grid square (e.g. a figure of 5 means the location is halfway across the grid square). Then follow the same procedure for the second

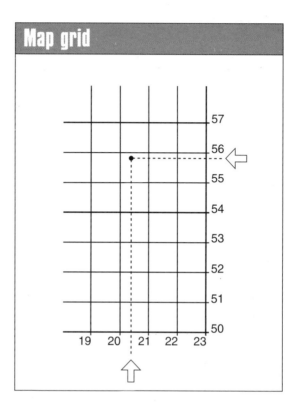

Map grid

half of the grid reference along the vertical grid line. See the example above of 204559.

Contours

A contour is usually a brown/orange line on a map that joins areas of the same height. It is a useful way of gauging the lie of the land. There are other ways of showing elevation, such as hachures (short parallel lines), hill shading and layer tints, but these are not as accurate as contours. In addition to contour lines, the map reader can use spot heights and trig points (see below), and conventional signs to judge elevation.

Contour lines on a map are always the same distance apart, e.g. 30ft (10m). The spacing of contour lines indicates the nature of the slope. Evenly spaced and wide apart lines (A): a gentle, uniform slope; evenly spaced and close together (B): a uniform, steep slope; and a ticked contour (C): a vertical or near vertical slope.

Other points to note about contours are:

- They always form a v-shape when they cross a river.
- They will not show every regularity of the ground that is below the height of the vertical interval between the contours, i.e they won't show a change in height of 15ft (5m) if the contour spacing is 30ft (10m).
- A road or path along which a contour runs is likely to be level.

- A stream is always in a valley and a lake or pond in a depression.

Spot height

This is normally a black point on the map with a figure beside it showing the exact height above sea level at that point. It is not represented on the ground.

Trig point

A small triangle on the map with a dot in the centre shows the altitude as well as a location used in survey triangulations. Trig points are represented on the ground by small triangular concrete blocks, which can be seen as the tops of many major hills.

Contour lines

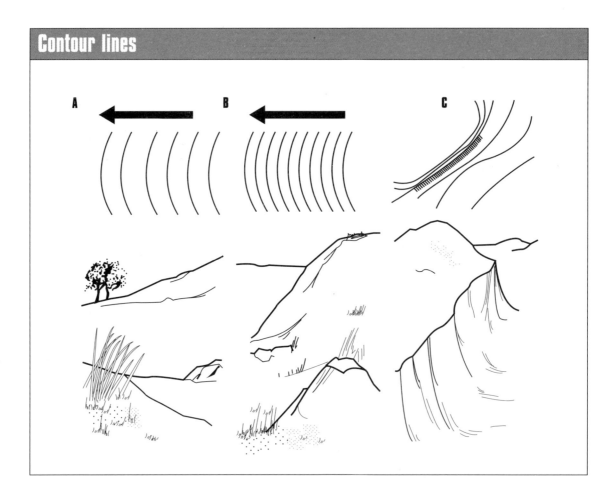

Cross-section

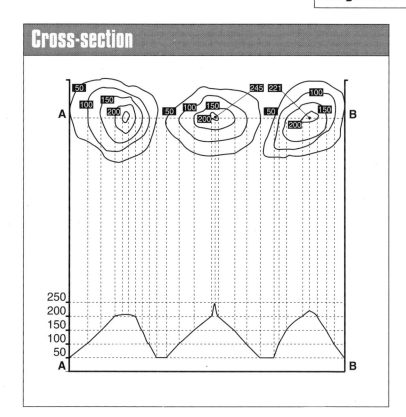

Drawing a cross-section of the ground between two points

Draw on your map a line of the ground you want to see in cross-section. Draw a second line, of the same length, horizontally on a piece of paper to represent ground level (A–B). Then, above and parallel to this ground level, draw lines to mark the contour heights, e.g. 50, 100, 150, etc. Mark every point on the map where the line crosses a contour, and transfer this data to your duplicate line on the paper. Raise a perpendicular line from each point to mark the appropriate height. Join up all these points to reveal a cross-section of the ground.

Contour lines and what they indicate

CONTOURS	TYPE OF SLOPE
Evenly spaced	Uniform
Close to each other	Steep
Far apart	Gentle
Varied spacing	Changeable
Close at foot of hill, wide at top	Convex
Far apart at foot, closer at top	Concave

Navigation with a Silva compass

Using a Silva compass, you can point the arrow on the front of the compass in the direction you wish to go. Then turn the dial so that the North mark is in line with the red compass needle. Your bearing will be shown by the black marker, in line with the direction-of-travel arrow. Holding the compass in front of you, it is relatively easy to stay on the correct bearing by keeping the marker of North on the compass lined up with the compass needle.

To work out your course from a map, place the side of your compass on a line between your position and your objective. Turn the compass dial until the marked orientating lines on the dial are parallel with the north–south lines on the map, with the orientating arrow pointing north. Note the reading on the marker line and then add the required number of mils for magnetic variation. The compass is now set on the correct bearing. When you take it off the map, you need only turn yourself, with the compass in front of you, until the red needle lies directly on North. You are then facing in the direction you wish to travel.

Finding your own position with map and compass

To determine your own position you can choose two landmarks which will be marked on the map, such as a hill or cairn. Point the arrow on the front of the compass at the first landmark and turn the bowl until the North mark on the compass is lined up with the red compass needle. Note the bearing and subtract the correct number of mils for magnetic variation.

Place the side of the compass on the landmark on the map and turn the compass base until the orientating lines in the base of the compass dial are lined up with the north–south grid lines, with the orientating arrow pointing north. Draw a line along the compass base from the landmark.

Repeat the procedure for the second landmark and find your position from where the lines intersect.

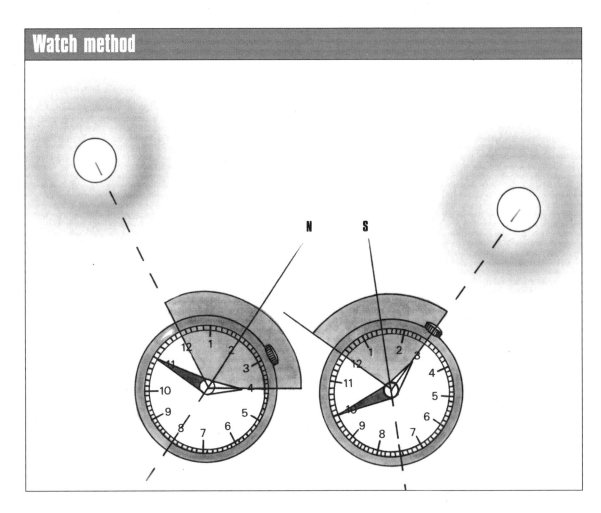

Watch method

NAVIGATION WITHOUT MAP OR COMPASS

There are a variety of navigation aids, some of which are more reliable than others. It is a good idea to work on the evidence of more than one aid before coming to any firm conclusions.

Sun

The sun rises in the east and sets in the west. At midday in the northern hemisphere the sun is due south, and due north in the southern hemisphere.

Watch

In the northern hemisphere, hold the watch with the hour hand pointing to the sun. Imagine a line travelling through the 12, and true south is midway between the hour hand and the 12.

In the southern hemisphere, point the imaginary line through 12 o'clock at the sun, and true north is the mid point between the 12 and the hour hand.

Time and direction by shadow

Place the stick at the intersection of the east–west line and the north–south line.

Time and direction by shadow

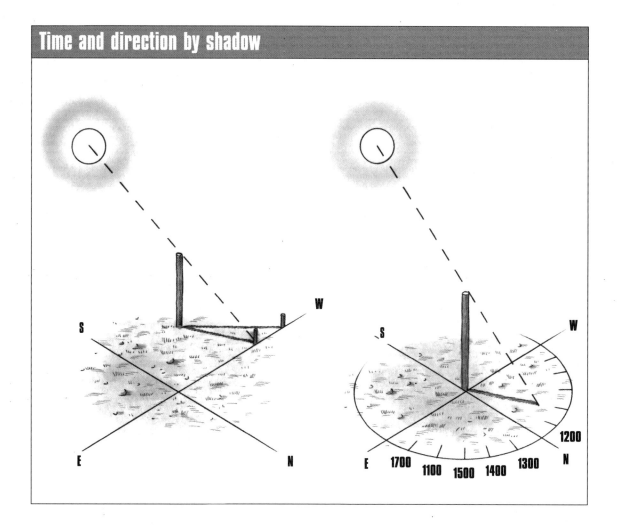

Stick and shadow method

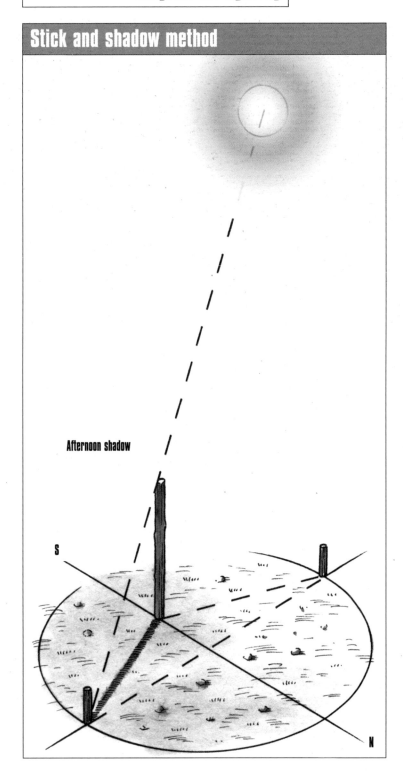

Afternoon shadow

S

N

Regardless of where you are, the west part of the east-west line shows 0600 hours and the east part 1800 hours. The north-south line becomes the noon line and the shadow of the stick becomes the hour hand.

Stick and shadow
East-west line:
Put a stick about 3ft (1m) high into the ground, which should be flat and clear of debris. Mark the tip of the shadow with a stone. Ten minutes later mark it again. The straight line between these points marks the east-west line.

North-south line:
Put a stick about 2ft (0.5m) high into flat ground. With a piece of string, stretched from the stick, draw an arc round the base of the stick, the same radius as the shadow. When the shadow touches the arc again, mark it with a stone or peg. Divide the angle formed by the base of the stick and the two pegs. This will indicate south in the northern hemisphere and north in the southern hemisphere.

Stars
Northern hemisphere
The North Star or Polaris can be found by following the Plough, Cassiopea and Orion.

Southern hemisphere
Multiply the longest axis of

Pole star

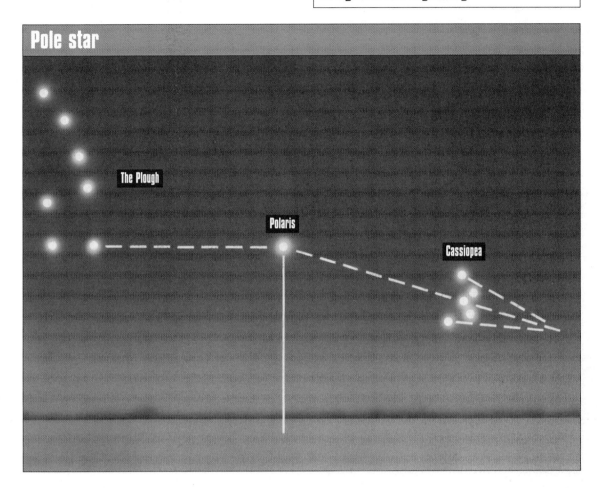

The Plough

Polaris

Cassiopea

the southern cross by 4.5, which brings you to an imaginary point above the horizon. Your southern landmark will be immediately below the point.

Star movement

Set your eyes on two fixed points on the ground in the distance to help you observe the movements of a star. Look at the star above the points on the ground. If after a period, the star appears to be rising, you are looking approximately due east. If the star is falling, you are looking approximately due west. If it loops towards the right, you are looking approximately due south, and if it loops towards the left, you are looking approximately due north.

Plants

You will need practice and experience to draw accurate conclusions about direction from plant growth, and always take as wide a sample as possible. Back up the evidence with other means. Certain rules can be followed:

- Flowers tend to grow towards the sun.
- The foliage of trees will be most abundant on the sunny side.
- Moss tends to grow on the damper side of a tree, i.e. the side away from the sun, but this can be influenced by other factors.
- In the northern hemisphere, the rings of a tree stump will be closer together on the south side of the tree, and the bark will also tend to stretch more on the south side.

Travelling time and distance

IN IDEAL CONDITIONS WITH LITTLE LOAD

Miles	Minutes
3 miles (5km)	60
½ mile (1km)	12

TRAILS IN DAYLIGHT WITH LITTLE LOAD

Miles	Minutes
1¾ miles (3km)	60

NIGHT CLOUD AND MOONLESS NIGHT IN CLOSE COUNTRY WITH LOAD

Miles	Minutes
½ mile (1km)	60

HILLY COUNTRY IN DAYLIGHT WITH LOAD

Miles	Minutes
1½ miles (2.5km)	60

TROPICAL RAINFOREST IN DAYLIGHT

Miles	Minutes
½ mile (1km)	60

DECIDUOUS FOREST IN DAYLIGHT

Miles	Minutes
¼ mile (0.5km)	60

TALL GRASS

Miles	Minutes
¼ mile (0.5km)	60

Improvised compass needle

You can magnetise a needle by stroking it with a magnet or a piece of silk, repeating the process every few hours to keep it magnetised. Hang the magnetised needle freely from a piece of thread, making sure there are no twists in the thread to influence the needle. The needle should point north.

DEAD RECKONING

This way of estimating distance that you travel involves plotting a series of points on your route with the help of a map, compass, protractor, route card and log.

Plot your route on the map, and mark out the distance and direction of each leg of the journey on the route card. When walking, keep a record of the bearing and distance covered in the log. If for any reason you have to change direction, record this in the log.

Work out your average pace, as this will help you to tell how far you have travelled. The average pace is 60–70 double paces per 32ft (100m) on flat easy ground. You will need to have an idea of the difference in your pace when walking uphill, and also the kind of terrain you are crossing. If you are walking on slippery ground or have shoes with poor traction, you will tend to take shorter paces.

SIGNALLING

Signalling will make a great deal of difference to your chances of survival if you can communicate effectively, for example to a passing aeroplane. It may be your first and last chance. You do not want to wave frantically at an aircraft only to see the pilot give a friendly wave back and then disappear over the horizon.

In this section you can learn a few of the internationally accepted signals that will be instantly recognized by potential rescuers, and also ways to make sure they are likely to be seen. You will need to find the highest and flattest area on which to make your signal.

Body signals

These should be made in such a way as to make it obvious to a pilot in an aeroplane or helicopter precisely what you are communicating. If the pilot has understood your message he will either tilt his wings or flash green signal lights. If he has not understood, he will encircle the aircraft or flash red signal lights.

Body signals

Our receiver is operating

Affirmative (yes)

Can proceed shortly, wait if practicable

Need mechanical help or parts, long delay

Do not attempt to land here

Pick us up, aircraft abandoned

Use drop message

All ok, do not wait

Negative

Land here (point in direction of landing)

Need medical assistance URGENTLY

Ground to air signals

1. —
2. ☰
3. ✕
4. F
5. V
6. □

7. — —
8. K
9. →
10. I >
11. L ˥
12. △

13. L
14. LL
15. N
16. Y
17. ⌐L
18. W

1. Need doctor – serious injuries
2. Need medical supplies
3. Unable to proceed
4. Need food and water
5. Need firearms and ammunition
6. Need map and compass
7. Need signal lamp with battery and radio
8. Indicate direction to proceed
9. Am proceeding in this direction
10. Will attempt take-off
11. Aircraft seriously damaged
12. Probably safe to land here
13. Need food and oil
14. All well
15. No
16. Yes
17. Not understood
18. Need engineer

Morse code

A . _	M _ _	Y _ . _ _
B _ . . .	N _ .	Z _ _ . .
C _ . _ .	O _ _ _	1 . _ _ _ _
D _ . .	P . _ _ .	2 . . _ _ _
E .	Q _ _ . _	3 . . . _ _
F . . _ .	R . _ .	4 . . . . _
G _ _ .	S . . .	5 . . . . .
H	T _	6 _ . . . .
I . .	U . . _	7 _ _ . . .
J . _ _ _	V . . . _	8 _ _ _ . .
K _ . _	W . _ _	9 _ _ _ _ .
L . _ . .	X _ . . _	0 _ _ _ _ _

Signalling equipment

Red parachute rocket
Hand flares (pin point red)
Buoyant orange smoke
Sea-dye markers
Signal pistol
Signalling torch
Heliograph
Personal locator beacon
VHF rescue radio
Whistle
Mirror

Radio

If you have access to a radio, your chances of rescue are greatly improved. Make sure you know how to use any available radios on an expedition. If you make contact on the radio, it is important that you use the following sequence:

- Mayday, Mayday.
- Your call sign (if you have one).
- Your name.
- Your location (grid reference).
- Number of survivors.
- Grid references of available landing sites.
- Inform them if you need special medical help.

Listen carefully to instructions from rescuers at all stages.

Fire

Three fires in a triangle is an internationally recognised distress signal. They can also be in a straight line with about an 80ft (25m) gap. It is difficult to maintain three fires over a long period, so if necessary have one burning and two more ready to light if required.

Mirror

This can also be a suitably burnished shiny object, like the inside lid of your survival tin. A reflected signal can be seen for up to 62 miles (100km) in normal conditions, and up to 100 miles (160km) in the desert. Take care not to flash it for too long into the cockpit of a nearby aircraft as it can blind the pilot.

Natural signals

In snow you can make a shadow SOS signal by kicking a path in the shape of the letters in the snow. The letters should be about 40ft (12m) high and you can build ridges to emphasise the shadow effect. You can also trace out letters with boughs, or logs.

A single tree can be set alight and turned into a burning torch. Make sure it is not near other trees that will catch alight.

Pyrotechnics

Since you are likely to have a limited supply of pyrotechnics, it is best to use them with care, and only when you consider they are likely to be seen by a passing aircraft. An aircraft using the Night Search Technique will fire green flares every 5–10 minutes. If you see one or more of these flares, wait for the aircraft to be clear of the glare of its own flares and then fire a red flare, followed by a second flare after a short interval. The aircraft will turn towards the first flare if it is seen and check its course on the second one, firing a succession of green lights until it is overhead. Wait for the aircraft to be overhead and then fire a third flare. You can also fire the third flare if you think the aircraft is going off course.

Handle flares with great care. Hold them at arm's length and at shoulder height, and make sure they are not pointing at anyone or anything. A hand-held flare should have a cap that should be removed before removing the base cap, which will expose a short string or other safety device. Make sure the flare is pointing up and away before pulling the string or other firing device. Prepare yourself for the recoil from the flare as it ignites. A flare may become hot – make sure you do not drop it on anything that will catch fire, or into the bottom of a lifeboat.

Lights

If you are using signal lights, send six flashes in one minute, then allow one minute's pause. Then send six more flashes, and so on. A green light from an aircraft will mean message understood. A red flare indicates distress. A white flare acknowledges or warns.

Sound

If you are using sound, send six signal blasts in one minute, then allow one minute's pause, then six more blasts, and so on. Sound carries further at dusk.

Phonetic alphabet

A	Alpha	N	November
B	Bravo	O	Oscar
C	Charlie	P	Papa
D	Delta	Q	Quebec
E	Echo	R	Romeo
F	Foxtrot	S	Sierra
G	Golf	T	Tango
H	Hotel	U	Unicorn
I	India	V	Victor
J	Juliet	W	Whisky
K	Kilo	X	X-ray
L	Lima	Y	Yankee
M	Mike	Z	Zulu

If an aircraft rocks from side to side, it means 'message understood'. If it circles to the right, it means it does not understand the message.

Mountain rescue code
SOS
Flare signal   Red
Sound signal   3 short blasts, 3 long, 3 short
Light signal   3 short flashes, 3 long, 3 short

Help needed
Flare signal   Red
Sound signal   6 blasts in quick succession
Light signal   6 flashes in quick succession

Message understood
Flare signal   White
Sound signal   3 flashes in quick succession
Light signal   3 flashes in quick succession

Return to base
Flare signal   Green

Sound signal   Prolonged succession of blasts
Light signal   Prolonged succession of flashes

Helicopter rescue
Requirements to land

- A flat clear surface with a gradient of no more than 7° (1 in 10) on which to land.
- Clear the site of anything that is likely to be blown up by the downdraught from the helicopter blades, such as loose snow and leaves.
- Mark the landing point with an H made out of flattened rocks or some firmly anchored material.
- At night, shine torch beams into the sky to attract attention, then down onto the landing point. Do not point them into the pilot's eyes.
- When the helicopter lands, do not approach from the rear as you can get hit by the rear rotor blades.

CHAPTER TWELVE

Rafts and River Crossings

To be able either to cross a river safely or to float downstream on a raft to find human habitation are important skills for the survivor. But the dangers should never be underestimated.

All moving bodies of water should be treated with great respect. You can be in danger of being swept off your feet by the current or of falling off a raft, of being dangerously affected by the cold or of being caught in some obstacle like a fallen tree.

RAFTS
Log Raft

A raft can be constructed from suitable logs – test them to make sure they float (at least half in the water and half out). When tying the logs together, make sure you cut deep notches into the logs so that the rope or other material you are using to bind them does not slip under the twisting action that will take place in the water. You can float the logs in the water (making sure they are tied to the land) to see what their natural flotation properties are, i.e. which side will be submerged and which side will form the deck.

Place the logs over two cross-bars at either end, with the longest log at the centre and place the next size down on either side symmetrically, so that you have some kind of prow on the raft. Lash the main logs together and then place two bars across the

Raft

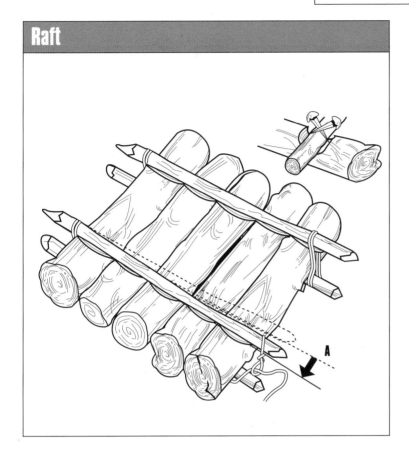

raft at both ends above the other bars. Cut notches in these bars and then lash them together to create pressure on the sides. You can add more cross-bars to form a flatter deck, according to how much time you have and how detailed you require the construction to be.

Centre boards, which will act like keels and help to stop the raft drifting sideways, can be pushed down between gaps in the logs and securely lashed. As in all survival matters, you can improvise according to your needs and the available materials.

Raft steering

You can construct an A-frame at the back of the raft to hold a steering oar, but the A-frame will need to be firmly constructed and lashed if it is not to collapse. Alternatively,

you can use a simpler method, which is to build up the rear of the raft with another couple of logs and then fix the steering oar on top of these in such a way that you will be able to turn it without losing it in the water (A).

Bamboo raft

You can cut 10ft (3m) lengths of bamboo (the number will depend on the number of people using the raft). If you use about 12 lengths, side by side, the raft should be able to take up to four people. In the penultimate bamboo section at each end, cut a hole so that a cross stake can pass through all the lengths of bamboo lying side by side. Each bamboo cane should then be lashed to the cross stakes. You can then construct a second layer to form a platform, ideally with longer arms on the outside so that the platform can be more easily lashed to the bottom layer. The platform will give the raft depth and improve its flotation.

Brush raft

Take two ponchos and tie off the necks with the drawstring. Attach ropes to the corners and sides of the ponchos. Spread the poncho on the ground and pile fresh brush onto it to a height of 18ins (45cm). Pull the poncho neck drawstring up through the centre of the brush stack. Take two saplings and make an X-frame. Place the X-frame on top of the brush stack. Tie it in place with the central poncho neck-drawstrings. Pile another 18ins (45cm) of brush on top of this. Pull the poncho sides up around the brush and tie the ropes diagonally across, from corner to corner, and from side to side.

Spread the second poncho, hood up, next to the bundle. Roll the bundle into the centre of the second poncho, tied side-down. Tie the second poncho around the bundle with diagonal ropes and from side to side.

Log flotation

This simple but effective device can be made quickly with two light logs and some rope or similar material. Place the logs about 2ft (0.6m) apart and tie them together, preferably with notches in the logs so that the rope does not slip off. You should then be able to sit between the two logs, with your legs folded over one and your lower back lying against the other. Test the device to make sure your measurements are right and that it works before using it in deeper water. You can improvise other flotation devices, depending on your requirements and the materials available.

RIVER CROSSINGS

You will need to choose a suitable spot to cross a river. Look out for:

- A place where you are least in danger of losing your footing.
- Easy access to the water on one side and a way out on the other side.
- Safety from any dangerous wildlife.
- A good vantage point, by climbing a tree if necessary, so that you can plan your crossing.
- Currents. Make allowances for being carried downstream by the current and

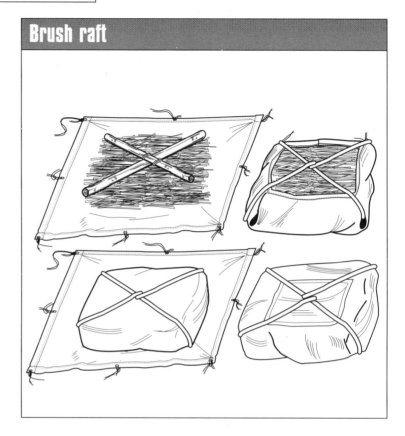

Brush raft

for missing your ideal landing spot.
- Where the water is shallowest, or where the river is divided up into separate channels that can be negotiated individually, or where there are natural stepping stones.
- Areas to avoid, such as where water is running rapidly over rocks, or where water eddies show that there is an obstacle under water that is creating dangerous back currents.
- Estuaries, which you also want to avoid. They can be wide and prone to awkward tide movements.

Wading across

Take your clothes off and store them in a plastic bag in your backpack. Keep your boots on to improve traction on the river bed. Ensure that your backpack can be easily unhitched from your back if you slip – do not have any buckles holding it on to your body. Hitch it over the downstream shoulder only. Take a sturdy pole with you and push it into the river bed upstream in order to help break the current. You can brace yourself against the pole. Cross the river at an angle of 45° to the current.

Roped crossing for three or more people

A roped crossing requires a loop of rope about three times as long as the width of the stream. The strongest person should go across first, with the rope tied round his/her chest. The other two let out the rope, making sure it does not snag on any obstacles, ready to haul the first person back if necessary.

When across, number one unties himself/herself and number two ties the rope round the chest. That person's crossing is monitored by rope holders on both banks. Number three then crosses, with one person holding the rope taut on the opposite side, and the other ready to help pull the rope if necessary.

Roped crossing

The strongest person goes ahead and ties the rope to a tree or other firm anchor on the far bank. The rest of the team follow, for example by hitching a karabiner with a chest harness on to the rope. The back packs can be brought across in a similar way. The last person swims across, with other team members ready to haul him/her in.

Swimming

Do not try swimming unless you are confident you can manage the current (throw bits of wood into the river to test the strength of the current), or that it is not too cold and that you will not be tangled up in weed, branches or other obstacles that may be in the river.

You will want to keep your clothes dry, so think of how you can create a waterproof flotation device that you can hold in front of you as you swim, kicking with your legs. Use flotation devices, such as the brush raft described above, or anything else that will float, to help you cross.

International grades of water difficulty

Grade 1   Moving water with ripples and small waves. Few obstructions.
Suitable for rafts.

Grade 2   Easy rapids with waves up to 3ft (1m) high. Some manoeuvering required
for a canoe.

Grade 3   Rapids with high waves.

Grade 4   Long difficult rapids which are largely unnavigable by open canoes.

Grade 5   Violent rapids.

Grade 6   Very dangerous.

NB. In a raft, anything beyond Grade 1 will probably be unsuitable, and the raft will need to be either carried or abandoned.

CHAPTER THIRTEEN

Ropes and Knots

As every Boy Scout and Girl Scout knows, ropes and knots are very important in almost any outside activity that involves construction, including shelters and rafts.

You may need to tie knots or use lashings in a variety of instances, such as for abseiling or constructing a raft. The following pages will provide guidelines on the most common knots and lashings and it is highly recommended that you practise tying a few of them before you set out on an expedition.

ROPES

It is encouraging for the survivalist without modern equipment to know that rope, cord and string used to be made entirely out of natural materials such as plant-stems and stalks. Plants from which they were made included cotton, sisal and hemp. If you are caught without a rope, therefore, you can go a long way by improvising with the natural fibres around you.

Although natural materials are still used today, they are generally weaker than modern man-made fibres, which include polyester, nylon, polypropylene and aramid fibres.

Rope care

If the rope gets wet, make sure that it dries slowly. Keep the rope as clean as possible

Knot strengths

(unknotted rope = 100 per cent)

KNOT	PERCENTAGE STRENGTH
Figure-of-eight	75–80
Bowline	70–75
Double fisherman's knot	65–70
Fisherman's knot	60–65
Clove hitch	60–65
Overhand	60–65

Terms of the knot

Bight	loop or bend
Working end	the end of the rope you are working with
Standing part	the part that the loop or bend is made round

Making cord

If you have caught any large game you can use the tendons to make sinew for lashing. Dry the tendons and then smash them into fibres. Moisten these and twist them into a strand, which can be braided if necessary. Plant fibres taken from the inner bark of some trees can also be used. Their strength will be increased by braiding.

Rawhide will make even stronger lashing material and is made from animal skin. Remove fat and meat from the skin and leave

and especially clear of anything abrasive. Make sure that the rope is not constantly rubbing against an object in the same place – spread the wear.

Rope strengths

	POLYPROPYLENE	POLYETHYLENE	NYLON	POLYESTER	SISAL
ABRASION RESISTANCE	Average	Good	Good	Very good	Poor
STRENGTH	Good	Average	Very good	Average	Poor
ELONGATION	Medium	Low	Very high	Low	Low
GENERAL	Good general-purpose rope, which is not affected by water or chemicals.	This has better abrasion resistance than polypropylene, though it is not as strong. Does not absorb water.	Strong, with excellent shock absorption. Break load is reduced when wet.	Retains strength when wet as well as flexibility.	Good quality natural fibre which should not be used in wet conditions.

to dry. When it is dry, cut it in a circular motion, to gain the maximum length from the available skin, at about ¼ins (6mm) thickness. Soak it for a couple of hours until it is soft and use when supple.

KNOTS

The definition of a knot is that it secures two ends of the same material, or that it is used to tie small material like string or angler's line. A bend is a knot that joins two separate ropes or other bits together. A hitch is used to attach a line to a rail, a post, a ring or onto another rope.

Remember that a knot is the weakest part of the rope when it is tied, and will make the rope even weaker if it is not tied properly.

Types of knots
Overhand knot
Make a loop and pass the working end back through it.

Double overhand knot
This is the same as the overhand knot but the working end is taken twice round the ropes before being fed through.

Reef knot
This should not be used for major work with ropes, but is useful in tying bits of string or cord together for lighter work. The principle is 'left over right and right over left'. The loops should then slide over each other.

To make it doubly secure, make a half hitch with the working ends on both sides of the knot.

Fisherman's knot
This is a useful way to join two similar ropes. Lay the two ropes parallel to each other. Tie

Sheet bend

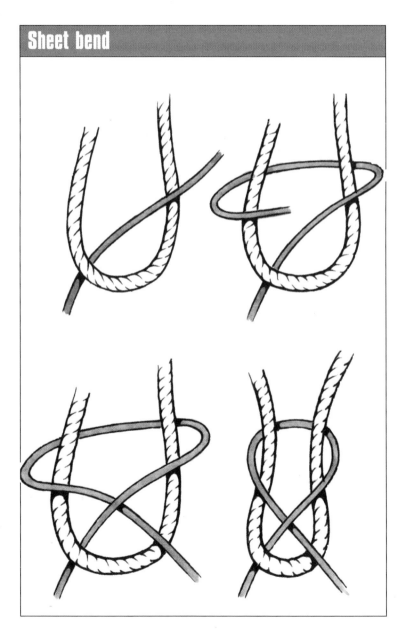

an identical overhand knot round each standing part with the other working end, and then pull them together.

Double fisherman's knot
A more secure method of joining two ropes, this involves tying two double overhand knots round each rope and pulling tight.

Figure-of-eight
This can be used for tying into a rope or for anchoring somebody. It should be easy to untie even when wet, although natural fibres can tend to jam when wet. Take the working part across the front of the standing part, then round and across the back. Bring the end forward and pass it through the loop.

Sheet bend
This can be used for tying ropes of unequal size together, but it can tend to jam and it is not among the strongest of knots. Make a loop near the end of the rope, with the short end on the right. Pass the end of the second rope up through the loop, round the back from right to left, and then tuck through its own standing part.

Double sheet bend
This is more secure and it requires an extra turn through the tuck.

Carrick bend
This knot is often used for joining larger ropes and cables. Weave the ropes over and under in such a way that the working ends come out on opposite sides of the knot. Pull the knot tight.

LOOP MAKING
The bowline knot and its variants are some of the most widely used loop knots, largely because they are relatively simple to tie and have a high level of security. The bowline itself is also extremely easy to untie. Like all

knots, the bowline knots require practice to make for best use.

Bowline
This has a wide range of uses and is often used by climbers for tying on. Decide how large you want your loop to be, allow three times the length of the loop, lead the end of the rope up through the loop, around the back of the standing part and back down through the loop (A).

Triple bowline
This is made with a double rope. First, make a loop and then pass the double working ends through the loop, behind the standing part and back through the loop. This can be used for such requirements as forming a boatswain's chair or a chest harness (B).

Bowline in the bight
This has been used for such tasks as lowering an injured person, since the loops are designed so that they will not tighten when, for example, legs are put through them. This knot is usually tied in the middle of the rope, using a doubled end in the early stages. The first two stages are the same as for tying an ordinary bowline. Form a loop and pass the live end through it, then back down and up round the entire length of the knot before tightening it (C).

HITCHES
Half hitch
This offers no security when used on its own, but is often used as a step in making other knots. Place the rope round a bar or through a ring, both ends towards you. Take the short end across and round the standing part and up through the hole you have formed.

Timber hitch
As above, but take the working end round itself once more. Make sure the turns are taken round the working end itself so that the knot will tighten correctly.

Double sheet bend

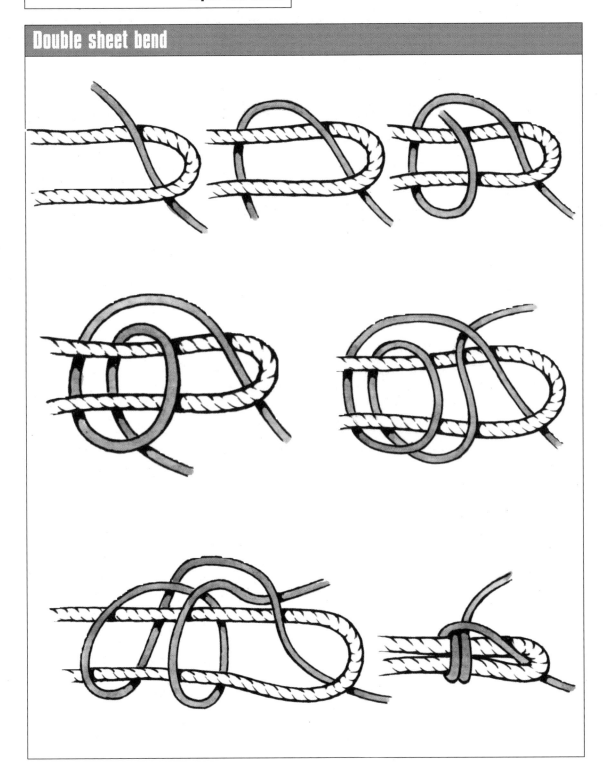

Loop making

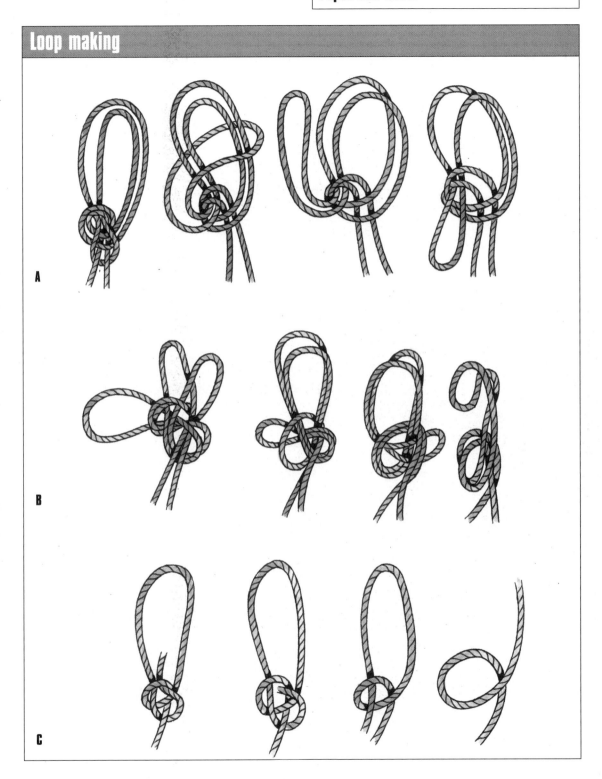

A

B

C

Timber hitch

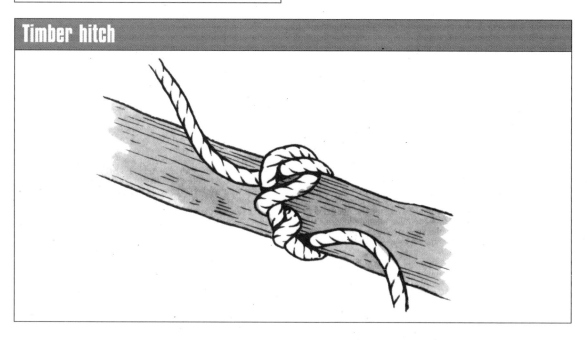

Clove hitch

This is a useful knot for attaching rope to a pole or ring, however it works best when the pull is at 90° to the object it is tied to, and it can work loose if pulled laterally. It can tend to jam when wet. Pass the working end over and round the bar. Then bring it across itself and round the bar again. Take the working end up and under itself, moving in the opposite direction to the standing end. Pull it tight.

Round turn and two half hitches

Used for securing a line to a rail, ring or bar. A turn consists of wrapping the rope 360° round a bar so that the end points in the same direction that it was pointing before the turn. This can be used to add extra friction when taking the strain on

Clove hitch

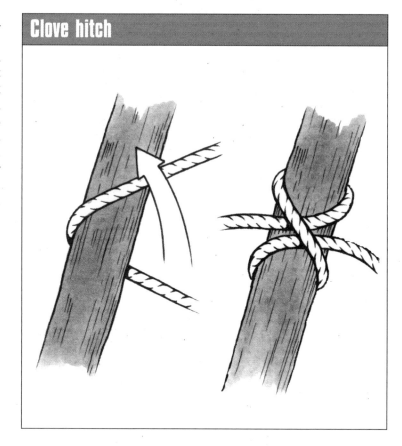

Round turn and two half hitches

crosspiece will be located. Take the rope round three or four turns on the outside of each previous turn. Take the rope over and under both poles anti-clockwise three or four times. Then make a full turn round a pole and a circuit in the opposite direction. End with a clove hitch on the pole where the lashing was started.

Diagonal lashing
This is an alternative to the square lashing and can be used when the two poles

something and paying out the line slowly.

A round turn is a turn-and-a-half, resulting in both ends pointing in the same direction, which gives even more friction and therefore control than a turn. If you add two half hitches, you have achieved this knot, which is often used for tying up boats to a post or bollard.

LASHINGS
Use lashings for constructing shelters, rafts and other structures, or for making equipment.

Square lashing
You can use this to secure two poles or logs at right angles to each other. Tie a clove hitch immediately under the place where the

Square lashing

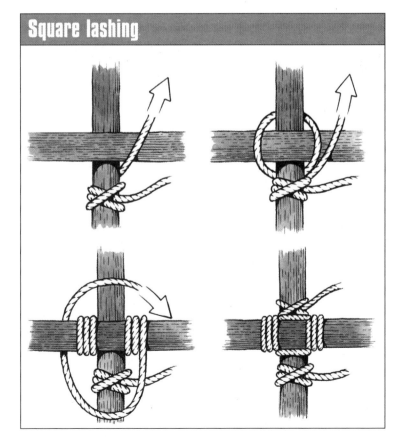

Diagonal lashing

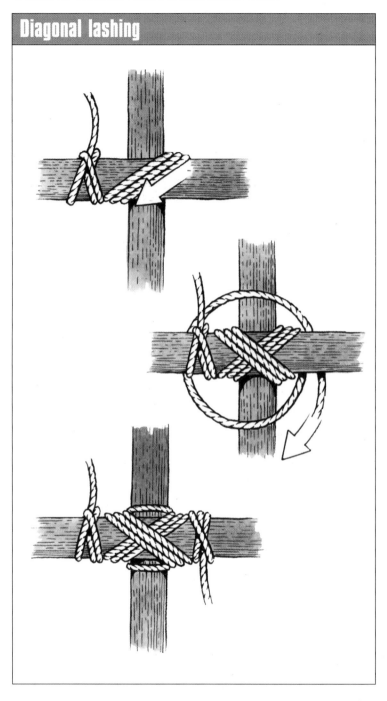

making sure that the turns are adjacent but not on top of each other. Take three more turns crosswise over the first turns. Pull them tight. Make two diagonal turns between the two logs, round the lashing turns. End with a clove hitch round the pole that the lashing started on.

Shear lashing

This can be used to tie the ends of two poles at an angle, for example when constructing an A-frame. Start with a clove hitch round one pole. Take seven or eight turns round both poles, laid side by side. Bringing the rope between the bars, frap a few times round the binding. End with a clove hitch on the pole opposite to the one which you started the lashing on. Pull the feet of the poles apart to tighten the lashing, and ensure the feet are embedded to stop them slipping apart.

You can use a similar method for three poles, making sure you frap on bindings in the two gaps.

Round lashing

Use this to lash two poles together alongside each other. Start with a clove hitch round both poles and then bind the rope round them. End with a clove hitch at the other end of the knot. You can force a wedge down between the lashing and the poles to make the lashing tighter.

are under strain and need pulling together. Tie a clove hitch round the two poles where they cross. Take three turns round both logs,

Shear lashing

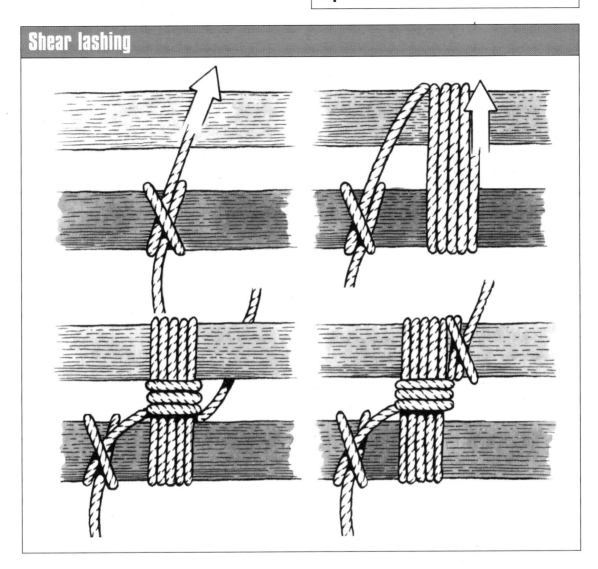

Round lashing

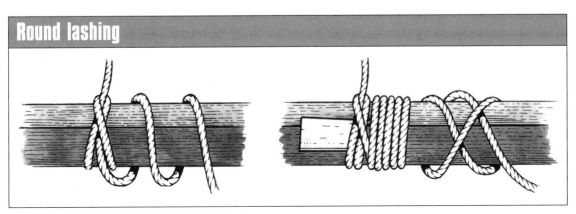

Foreign Travel

Travel abroad demands plenty of preparation, even when going a straightforward trip to somewhere in North America or Europe. If you are travelling further afield you will not only need to carry out the standard checks for essential documents but also be aware of the potential problems and restrictions that could be caused by unstable political regimes, wars and inadequate emergency services. You should take care to respect local customs, especially with regard to accepted standards of dress. There may be a high risk of diseases such as malaria and cholera and you should always take care with local drinking water. Remember that in many countries you may be required to produce personal identification on the spot.

Travel checklist

PASSPORT:	does it require renewal?
VISA:	some countries will turn you back if you do not have one
TRAVEL INSURANCE:	highly advisable for most destinations
MEDICAL INSURANCE:	highly advisable
INOCULATIONS:	against malaria, typhoid, dengue fever, etc
TRAVELLERS' CHEQUES:	as a security
FUNDS:	bank transfers can be lengthy and bureaucratic abroad, especially when you are not familiar with the language
CLOTHES:	if visiting a Muslim country you will be expected to respect local customs

1. ASIA

This is the largest continent, with a total area of about 17,226,000 square miles (44,614,000 square km). It comprises the eastern four fifths of the Eurasian land-mass. The Asian coastline is about 39,000 square miles (62,800 square km). It is the most highly populated continent at over 3 billion, though large areas of central and north Asia have a relatively low population density.

Afghanistan

CAPITAL: Kabul
TRAVEL TIPS: check before travelling about the current state of political unrest, about dangers to overflying civilian airliners and whether or not there is consular representation in the country.

Armenia

CAPITAL: Yerevan
TRAVEL TIPS: check on current state of internal affairs; a visa is normally required; take care with regard to standard of driving in the country.

Azerbaijan

CAPITAL: Baki (Baku)
TRAVEL TIPS: a visa is normally required; be extra vigilant if walking alone especially at night.

Bangladesh

CAPITAL: Dhaka
TRAVEL TIPS: beware of dangers of organised crime and of the poor state of some roads.

Bhutan

CAPITAL: Thimphu
TRAVEL TIPS: a visa is normally required; roads can be dangerous; take medical insurance; some religious establishments are off limits.

Brunei

CAPITAL: Bandar Seri Begawan
TRAVEL TIPS: strict laws in place with regard to drugs.

Burma

CAPITAL: Rangoon
TRAVEL TIPS: visitors are restricted to certain areas; do not photograph any kind of military installation; avoid large crowds/demonstrations; there are some dangers from the conflict between insurgents such as the Karen and the government.

Cambodia

CAPITAL: Phnom Penh
TRAVEL TIPS: beware of mines in some areas; avoid crowds/demonstrations; there can be severe floods in the rainy season.

China

CAPITAL: Beijing
TRAVEL TIPS: there has been an increase in criminal activity and there is some unrest, due in part to ethnic discontent and rising unemployment. There is some danger of earthquakes.

Georgia

CAPITAL: Tiblisi
TRAVEL TIPS: a visa is normally required; some areas are dangerous; roads can be poor; take care with drinking water etc.

India

CAPITAL: New Delhi
TRAVEL TIPS: disturbances in north-east and Kashmir should be avoided; driving can be poor; beware confidence tricksters.

Indonesia

CAPITAL: Jakarta
TRAVEL TIPS: check on latest political developments to gauge state of unrest; some anti-Western feeling due to East Timor crisis.

Iran

CAPITAL: Tehran
TRAVEL TIPS: dress modestly and take care to respect local customs in this respect; do not photograph military installations; ensure visa is up to date.

Iraq

CAPITAL: Baghdad
TRAVEL TIPS: do not visit unless given the all clear by your own government.

Israel

CAPITAL: Jerusalem
TRAVEL TIPS: keep up to date with political developments which could affect travel plans; there have been bombs on public transport; carry identification at all times.

Japan

CAPITAL: Tokyo
TRAVEL TIPS: Japan is a high-risk earthquake area.

Jordan

CAPITAL: Amman
TRAVEL TIPS: Although there is a peace treaty with Israel, there is much opposition to this in Jordan. Potential problems with terrorism mean that travellers should keep up to date with developments.

Kazakhstan

CAPITAL: Almaty (Alma Ata)
TRAVEL TIPS: a visa is normally required; it is advisable for Westerners to travel in groups as they can be targets of robberies; travel to neighbouring states can be difficult.

Korea, North

CAPITAL: P'yongyang
TRAVEL TIPS: check on arrangements for representation by your government in this country.

Korea, South

CAPITAL: Seoul
TRAVEL TIPS: obtain update on political developments as there is tension between North and South Korea which could erupt.

Kuwait
CAPITAL: Al Kuwayt
TRAVEL TIPS: keep up to date
with political developments, due
to tensions with Iraq; keep away
from Iraq border; take care with
regard to unexploded shells, etc
which remain from the war.

Kyrgyzstan
CAPITAL: Bishkek
TRAVEL TIPS: a visa is normally
required and identification
should be carried at all times;
beware of robberies and muggings. Roads and transport can
be of poor quality.

Laos
CAPITAL: Viangchen (Vientiane)
TRAVEL TIPS: some areas are
dangerous for travel due to
attacks on foreigners and unexploded mines, etc. Ensure you
have proper medical advice,
innoculations and insurance.

Lebanon
CAPITAL: Beirut
TRAVEL TIPS: keep up to date
with political developments in
the region; a visa is normally
required; travel is restricted to
certain areas, and take care not
to photograph any military
installations.

Malaysia
CAPITAL: Kuala Lumpur
TRAVEL TIPS: there are severe
laws against drugs; keep away
from crowds and demonstrations
of any kind; respect local customs
of decorum in dress, etc.

Mongolia
CAPITAL: Ulaanbaatar
(Ulan Bator)
TRAVEL TIPS: entry into the
country normally only by air
and train; internal communica-
tions are poor.

Nepal
CAPITAL: Kathmandu
TRAVEL TIPS: check on state of
security of the region you are

visiting; beware robberies;
standard of driving and transport is poor; ensure you have all
the correct insurance.

Oman
CAPITAL: Masqat (Muscat)
TRAVEL TIPS: keep in touch
with developments in the
Middle East.

Pakistan
CAPITAL: Islamabad
TRAVEL TIPS: there is danger
from armed gangs in some
areas; travel can be risky; check
on latest political developments
and beware the tension with
India over Kashmir.

Philippines
CAPITAL: Manila
TRAVEL TIPS: this is an earthquake and high-risk typhoon
zone; carry identification; beware
travelling alone in remote areas;
do not fraternise with strangers;
beware of danger from Malaria
and take medical precautions.

Russia
CAPITAL: Moscow
TRAVEL TIPS: check on advisabil-
ity of travel in certain areas;
there can be unrest caused by
rival gangs; a visa is normally
required.

Saudi Arabia
CAPITAL: Riyadh
TRAVEL TIPS: it is forbidden to
import or use alcohol, religious
material or pork; dress codes
must be observed; check on the
political status in the region.

Singapore
CAPITAL: Singapore City
TRAVEL TIPS: there are strict
drug laws; there is some danger
of offshore piracy.

Sri Lanka
CAPITAL: Colombo
TRAVEL TIPS: there have been
bomb attacks; check on current
state of tension between Tamil

Tigers and security forces; do not
photograph military installations;
driving and roads are poor.

Syria
CAPITAL: Dimasha (Damascus)
TRAVEL TIPS: dress should
respect local religious laws; no
photography near military installations; a visa must be carried.

Taiwan
CAPITAL: T'ai-pei
TRAVEL TIPS: beware dangers
from earthquakes in this region.

Tajikistan
CAPITAL: Dushanbe
TRAVEL TIPS: check on security
position and obtain clearance
from your government before
travelling.

Thailand
CAPITAL: Bangkok
TRAVEL TIPS: drug laws are strictly enforced; beware dangers of
flooding in some areas; do not travel to remote border areas without
checking on the security situation.

Turkey
CAPITAL: Ankara
TRAVEL TIPS: take comprehen-
sive insurance; beware standard
of driving is poor.

Turkmenistan
CAPITAL: Ashkhabad
TRAVEL TIPS: a visa is normally
required; roads are poor; take
medical precautions and beware
unsafe drinking water.

United Arab Emirates
CAPITAL: Abu Dhabi
TRAVEL TIPS: check on regional
security before travel; dress and
behave with decorum.

Uzbekistan
CAPITAL: Tashkent
TRAVEL TIPS: roads are poor;
beware photographing sensitive
establishments; take adequate
medical insurance and
precautions.

Vietnam
CAPITAL: Hanoi
TRAVEL TIPS: some areas have unexploded mines, etc.; take adequate medical insurance and precautions; drug laws are strictly enforced.

Yemen
CAPITAL: Saní
TRAVEL TIPS: check on local security before travel and obtain clearance from your government.

2. AFRICA
The second-largest continent, with a total area of about 11,724,000 square miles (30,365,000 square kilometres), Africa has a coastline of 18,950 miles. Much of Africa is tropical, with the equator cutting the continent almost equally in two.

Algeria
CAPITAL: Algiers
TRAVEL TIPS: internal tensions have made this a high-risk zone; seek advice before attempting to travel.

Angola
CAPITAL: Luanda
TRAVEL TIPS: identification should be carried at all times; seek advice before attempting to travel to this country; make security arrangements if travel is necessary.

Benin
CAPITAL: Porto-Novo
TRAVEL TIPS: do not go out alone, especially at night.

Botswana
CAPITAL: Gaborone
TRAVEL TIPS: rising unemployment has led to some rioting.

Burkina Faso
Capital: Ouagadougou
Travel tips: take adequate medical precautions, especially with regard to cholera.

Burundi
CAPITAL: Bujumbura
TRAVEL TIPS: a visa is normally required; check on regional security before travel and obtain clearance from your government.

Cameroon
CAPITAL: Yaoundé
TRAVEL TIPS: take advice on regional security; take sensible medical precautions, especially with regard to malaria.

Central African Republic
CAPITAL: Bangui
TRAVEL TIPS: check on regional security before attempting travel; obtain clearance from your government; take sensible medical precautions, especially with regard to malaria.

Chad
CAPITAL: Ndjamena
TRAVEL TIPS: check internal security, especially in border areas before travelling; take medical precautions, especially with regard to malaria.

Comoros
CAPITAL: Moroni
TRAVEL TIPS: check on internal security before travelling; take medical precautions, especially with regard to cholera and malaria.

Congo, Republic of
CAPITAL: Brazzaville
TRAVEL TIPS: tensions and violence between government and militias make it advisable to check on internal security before travelling and obtain clearance from your government if travel is absolutely necessary.

Côte D'Ivoire
CAPITAL: Yamoussoukro
TRAVEL TIPS: take sensible medical precautions before travelling; standard of driving and of roads is poor; beware dangerous bathing.

Djibouti
CAPITAL: Djibouti
TRAVEL TIPS: check on regional security before attempting travel; take sensible medical precautions.

Egypt
CAPITAL: Cairo
TRAVEL TIPS: check on regional security before travelling; dress and behave with decorum; beware unexploded landmines in some areas.

Equatorial Guinea
CAPITAL: Malabo
TRAVEL TIPS: beware walking alone after dark, and guard possessions carefully; take medical precautions with regard to malaria.

Eritrea
CAPITAL:Asmara
TRAVEL TIPS: check on regional security before attempting to travel; obtain clearance from your government if travel is absolutely necessary.

Ethiopia
CAPITAL: Addis Ababa
TRAVEL TIPS: a visa is normally required; check on regional security before attempting to travel.

Gabon
CAPITAL: Libreville
TRAVEL TIPS: take medical precautions with regard to malaria.

Gambia
CAPITAL: Banjul
TRAVEL TIPS: drug laws are strictly enforced; check on internal security before travelling; standards of driving and of roads are poor.

Ghana
CAPITAL: Accra
TRAVEL TIPS: take medical precautions with regard to malaria; standards of driving and of roads are poor.

Guinea

CAPITAL: Conakry
TRAVEL TIPS: take precautions with regard to malaria and other diseases; beware tensions, particularly in border areas.

Guinea-Bissau

CAPITAL: Bissau
TRAVEL TIPS: check on internal security before travelling; take medical precautions with regard to malaria and other diseases.

Kenya

CAPITAL: Nairobi
TRAVEL TIPS: beware high incidence of muggings; check on internal security before travelling; take medical precautions with regard to malaria, cholera and other diseases.

Lesotho

CAPITAL: Maseru
TRAVEL TIPS: check on internal security before travelling.

Liberia

CAPITAL: Monrovia
TRAVEL TIPS: check on internal security before travelling; obtain clearance from your government if travel is absolutely necessary.

Libya

CAPITAL: Tripoli
TRAVEL TIPS: be circumspect with regard to photography and local customs; alcohol is illegal.

Madagascar

CAPITAL: Antananarivo
TRAVEL TIPS: take medical precautions with regard to cholera.

Malawi

CAPITAL: Lilongwe
TRAVEL TIPS: beware robberies and muggings; don't fraternise with strangers; take medical precautions with regard to cholera and malaria, and beware contaminated drinking water.

Mali

CAPITAL: Bamako

TRAVEL TIPS: check on internal security before travelling; take sensible medical precautions.

Mauritania

CAPITAL: Nouakchott

Mauritius

CAPITAL: Port Louis
TRAVEL TIPS: take care with regard to local drug laws.

Morocco

CAPITAL: Rabat
TRAVEL TIPS: beware severe drug laws; avoid large gatherings; respect local religious customs.

Mozambique

CAPITAL: Maputo
TRAVEL TIPS: take medical precautions with regard to cholera and malaria, and beware contaminated drinking water; it is advisable to travel in groups; do not go out after dark; beware unexploded mines, etc.

Namibia

CAPITAL: Windhoek
TRAVEL TIPS: check on regional security before travelling; take medical precautions with regard to malaria.

Niger

CAPITAL: Niamey
TRAVEL TIPS: check on local and regional stability before travelling.

Nigeria

CAPITAL: Abuja
TRAVEL TIPS: check on internal security before travelling; beware armed robbery and local disturbances.

Rwanda

CAPITAL: Kigali
TRAVEL TIPS: check on potential dangers from rebels, especially in border regions.

Senegal

CAPITAL: Dakar
TRAVEL TIPS: beware of border region with Guinea-Bissau; take

medical precautions with regard to malaria.

Seychelles

CAPITAL: Victoria
TRAVEL TIPS: take normal precautions with regard to possessions and do not go out alone especially after dark.

Sierra Leone

CAPITAL: Freetown
TRAVEL TIPS: there has been hostage taking of foreigners; do not travel unless given clearance by your government.

Somalia

CAPITAL: Mogadishu
TRAVEL TIPS: check on internal security before attempting to travel to this country.

South Africa

CAPITAL: Pretoria & Cape Town
TRAVEL TIPS: beware that tourists are frequently targetted by pickpockets and there are also incidents of muggings and rape.

Sudan

CAPITAL: Khartoum
TRAVEL TIPS: check on internal security before travel; beware unexploded landmines, etc.

Swaziland

CAPITAL: Mbabane
TRAVEL TIPS: do not fraternise with strangers; beware of poor standards of roads and driving.

Tanzania

CAPITAL: Dodoma
TRAVEL TIPS: beware unrest in border areas; beware dangers of muggings and robberies; take medical precautions with regard to cholera and malaria, and beware contaminated drinking water.

Togo

CAPITAL: Lomé
TRAVEL TIPS: carry identification with you at all times.

Tunisia
CAPITAL: Tunis
TRAVEL TIPS: drug laws are
strictly enforced.

Uganda
CAPITAL: Kampala
TRAVEL TIPS: a visa is normally
required; obtain advice on which
areas to avoid due to risk from
bandits, local insurgents, etc.

Western Sahara
CAPITAL: Laâyoune
POLITICAL: Territory in dispute.
TRAVEL TIPS: check on local and
regional security before attempt-
ing to travel.

Zaire
CAPITAL: Kinshasa
TRAVEL TIPS: See Congo.

Zambia
CAPITAL: Lusaka
TRAVEL TIPS: a visa is normally
required; strict drug laws; take
medical precautions for cholera
and malaria, and beware contaminated drinking water.

Zimbabwe
CAPITAL: Harare
TRAVEL TIPS: beware petty
crime and poor standard of
roads and driving.

3. NORTH AND CENTRAL AMERICA
The third-largest continent
has an area of about 9,355,000
square miles (24,230,000
square km). Its coastline is
about 37,000 miles (95,829.5
square km).

Bahamas
CAPITAL: Nassau
TRAVEL TIPS: there is a risk of
hurricanes in this area.

Belize
CAPITAL: Belmopan
TRAVEL TIPS: take medical precautions, especially with regard
to cholera.

Canada
CAPITAL: Ottawa

Costa Rica
CAPITAL: San José

Cuba
CAPITAL: Havana
TRAVEL TIPS: drug laws are
strictly enforced; beware taking
photographs of sensitive
installations.

Dominican Republic
CAPITAL: Santo Domingo
TRAVEL TIPS: do not go out
alone after dark; take care with
drinking water.

El Salvador
CAPITAL: San Salvador
TRAVEL TIPS: beware robberies,
muggings and murders; take
care with drinking water.

Greenland
CAPITAL: Nuuk

Guatemala
CAPITAL: Guatemala City
TRAVEL TIPS: drug laws are
strictly enforced; beware robberies and muggings.

Haiti
CAPITAL: Port-au-Prince
TRAVEL TIPS: beware robberies
and muggings.

Honduras
CAPITAL: Tegucigalpa
TRAVEL TIPS: beware robberies
and muggings; take care with
drinking water; this is a high-risk
hurricane area.

Jamaica
CAPITAL: Kingston
TRAVEL TIPS: drug laws are
strictly enforced; beware travelling alone after dark/robberies.

Nicaragua
CAPITAL: Managua
TRAVEL TIPS: take medical
precautions with regard to
cholera and malaria, and beware

contaminated drinking water;
check on internal security, especially in border areas.

Panama
CAPITAL: Panama City
TRAVEL TIPS: beware unrest and
danger of kidnapping in border
areas.

United States
CAPITAL: Washington

4. SOUTH AMERICA
The fourth-largest continent
has an area of about
6,878,000 square miles
(17,814,000 square km) and
a coastline of about 15,800
miles (40,922 square km).

Argentina
CAPITAL: Buenos Aires
TRAVEL TIPS: beware street
crime/robberies, etc.

Bolivia
CAPITAL: La Paz/Sucre
TRAVEL TIPS: beware of health
difficulties caused by high altitude; beware street crime; drug
laws are strictly enforced.

Brazil
CAPITAL: Brasília
TRAVEL TIPS: take medical precautions, especially with regard
to cholera; beware street crime,
especially at night.

Chile
CAPITAL: Santiago
TRAVEL TIPS: keep abreast of
political developments in order
to assess risk.

Colombia
CAPITAL: Bogotá
TRAVEL TIPS: drug laws are
strictly enforced; check on internal security with regard to activities of guerrillas etc. before
internal travel.

Ecuador
CAPITAL: Quito
TRAVEL TIPS: this is a high-risk

volcano area; drug laws are strictly enforced; carry personal identification with you; take sensible medical precautions.

French Guiana
CAPITAL: Cayenne
TRAVEL TIPS: take medical precautions, particulary with regard to dengue and malaria.

Guyana
CAPITAL: Georgetown
TRAVEL TIPS: drug laws are strictly enforced; take sensible medical precautions, especially with regard to typhoid.

Paraguay
CAPITAL: Asunción
TRAVEL TIPS: keep up to date with internal and regional security; beware problems with insurgents in border areas.

Peru
CAPITAL: Lima
TRAVEL TIPS: beware of problems associated with high altitude; take medical precautions, particularly with regard to malaria; drug laws are strictly enforced; do not travel alone unless absolutely necessary.

Surinam
CAPITAL: Paramaribo
TRAVEL TIPS: keep up to date with internal tensions between authorities and ethnic groups; beware of drug laws.

Uruguay
CAPITAL: Montevideo
TRAVEL TIPS: beware street crime, and guard possessions carefully.

Venezuela
CAPITAL: Caracas
TRAVEL TIPS: high risk of mud slides and similar natural disasters; there has been a rise in crime and drug trafficking; beware problems with drug traffickers in border areas.

5. ANTARCTICA
The territorial claims of Argentina, Australia, Chile, France, Great Britain, New Zealand and Norway to parts of Antarctica have been put on ice ever since 1961 when an Antarctic Treaty was signed that asserted the preeminence of international cooperation in scientific research over political advantages. The total area of Antarctica is about 5,405,430 square miles (14,000,000 square km). The coastline is about 9702 miles (17,968 km).

6. EUROPE
The area of Europe is about 4,000,000 square miles (10,400,000 square km) with a coastline about 24,000 miles (38,000 km) long.

Albania
CAPITAL: Tirana
TRAVEL TIPS: keep up to date with internal and regional security; standards of driving and of roads are poor; take care with contaminated local drinking water.

Austria
CAPITAL: Vienna

Belarus
CAPITAL: Minsk
TRAVEL TIPS: a visa is normally required; take particular care with drinking water and food.

Belgium
CAPITAL: Brussels

Bosnia and Hercegovina
CAPITAL: Sarajevo
TRAVEL TIPS: beware unexploded mines, etc.

Bulgaria
CAPITAL: Sofia
TRAVEL TIPS: standards of roads

and of driving are poor.

Croatia
CAPITAL: Zagreb
TRAVEL TIPS: take advice on medical precautions; check on which areas to avoid due to risk from unexploded mines, etc.

Czech Republic
CAPITAL: Prague
TRAVEL TIPS: carry personal identification at all times; take advice on necessary medical precautions.

Denmark
CAPITAL: Copenhagen

Estonia
CAPITAL: Talinn
TRAVEL TIPS: personal identification must be carried at all times; standards of roads and of driving are poor.

Finland
CAPITAL: Helsinki

France
CAPITAL: Paris

F.Y.R.O.M (Macedonia)
CAPITAL: Skopje

Germany
CAPITAL: Berlin

Great Britain
CAPITAL: London

Greece
CAPITAL: Athens
TRAVEL TIPS:take out medical and travel insurance.

Hungary
CAPITAL: Budapest
TRAVEL TIPS: personal identification must be carried at all times.

Iceland
CAPITAL: Reykjavik
TRAVEL TIPS: vehicles should have snow tyres, and check on state of internal routes, which

may quickly become blocked with snow.

Ireland
CAPITAL: Dublin

Italy
CAPITAL: Rome
TRAVEL TIPS: check on state of volcanic activity in Mt Etna region.

Latvia
CAPITAL: Riga
TRAVEL TIPS: personal identification must be carried at all times; do not go out alone at night unless absolutely necessary.

Lithuania
CAPITAL: Vilnius
TRAVEL TIPS: do not go out after dark alone in poorly lit areas.

Moldova
CAPITAL: Kishinev
TRAVEL TIPS: a visa is normally required; take care with regard to drinking water; beware of crime/robberies, etc.

Netherlands
CAPITAL: Amsterdam

Norway
CAPITAL: Oslo

Poland
CAPITAL: Warsaw
TRAVEL TIPS: standards of roads and of driving are poor.

Romania
CAPITAL: Bucharest
TRAVEL TIPS: a visa is normally required; standards of roads and of driving are poor; do not hand over personal documents unless in a police station.

Slovakia
CAPITAL: Bratislava
TRAVEL TIPS: carry identification with you at all times.

Slovenia
CAPITAL: Ljubljana
TRAVEL TIPS: carry identification with you at all times.

Spain
CAPITAL: Madrid

Sweden
CAPITAL: Stockholm

Switzerland
CAPITAL: Bern

Ukraine
CAPITAL: Kiev
TRAVEL TIPS: a visa is normally required; carry identification with you at all times; beware drinking water.

7. AUSTRALASIA
Australia itself is the smallest continent with an area of about 3,000,000 square miles (8,000,000 square km). The coastline is 13,909 miles (25,760 km).

Australia
CAPITAL: Canberra
TRAVEL TIPS: beware flash floods and bush fires; do not travel alone after dark.

Papua New Guinea
CAPITAL: Port Moresby
TRAVEL TIPS: a visa is normally required; be extremely vigilant about possible attacks; this is a volcano high risk area.

New Zealand
CAPITAL: Wellington

Index

index